THE JOURNAL OF A CAVALRY OFFICER
IN THE CORUNNA CAMPAIGN

A CAVALRY OFFICER IN THE CORUNNA CAMPAIGN

1808–1809

THE JOURNAL OF CAPTAIN GORDON
OF THE 15TH HUSSARS

EDITED BY COLONEL H. C. WYLLY, C.B.

WITH PORTRAITS AND MAPS

The Naval & Military Press Ltd

Reproduced by kind permission of the Central Library,
Royal Military Academy, Sandhurst

Published by
The Naval & Military Press Ltd
Unit 10 Ridgewood Industrial Park,
Uckfield, East Sussex,
TN22 5QE England
Tel: +44 (0) 1825 749494
Fax: +44 (0) 1825 765701
www.naval-military-press.com
www.military-genealogy.com
www.militarymaproom.com

DEDICATED

BY PERMISSION

TO THE

OFFICERS, NON-COMMISSIONED OFFICERS, AND
MEN OF THE 15TH (THE KING'S) HUSSARS

CONTENTS

CONTENTS

CHAPTER IV

CHAPTER V

PORTRAIT AND MAPS

ix

INTRODUCTION

ALEXANDER GORDON, the writer of this journal, was born in 1781. He inherited the estate of Auchlunies and, subsequently, the estates of Ellon, in Aberdeenshire, from his father, the third Earl of Aberdeen, in succession to his half-brother, the Hon. William Gordon.

He was a pupil of the Rev. Sydney Smith. He entered the army in 1803, being on July 9 of that year appointed Cornet in the 15th Light Dragoons, becoming Lieutenant on January 22, 1805. Just three years later he obtained a company in the 3rd West India Regiment, which, however, he probably never joined, as almost immediately —on March 3, 1808—he was reappointed to a troop in his old regiment, now Hussars, with which he served during the campaign under

Sir John Moore. In March, 1811, Captain Gordon transferred to the 60th Foot, and retired by the sale of his commission on October 17. In 1847 he was awarded the Peninsular Medal with clasp for Sahagun.

He married in 1811 Albinia Louisa, daughter of Captain Richard Cumberland (a son of Richard Cumberland the dramatist) and Lady Albinia, daughter of the third Earl of Buckingham-shire.

Captain Gordon was a J.P. and Deputy-Lieutenant for Aberdeenshire ; he died in 1872.

His journal, now in the possession of his grandson, Mr. Arthur Gordon, C.M.G., of Ellon, seems to supply something that has up to the present time been wanting in the history of the Corunna campaign ; for though many diaries and journals have been published, they deal chiefly with the doings of the other arms, and we know but little of the work of the cavalry during the advance and retreat. The story of hardship, gallantry, and privation here set down has the advantage of

being related by an officer who belonged to an
arm the discipline of which remained unimpaired,
and to a Regiment which, throughout the retire-
ment, was always with the rear-guard.

The maps are from sketches executed by
Captain Gordon, and his portrait, which forms
the frontispiece, is from a miniature by Andrew
Robertson, now in the possession of the Hon.
Mrs. Richard Cavendish Boyle, Captain Gordon's
youngest daughter.

H. C. W.

September, 1913.

PREFACE

THE following narrative, comprising a journal of the disastrous campaign in Spain under Sir John Moore, was drawn up from notes taken on the spot, immediately after my return to England, while the occurrences it relates were still fresh in my memory. The details refer chiefly to the operations of my own corps, from which I was seldom absent; but during the retreat the troops were so much concentrated that regimental officers—those of the cavalry, at least—enjoyed opportunities of becoming acquainted with the situation and general movements of the army superior to those afforded by staff appointments in ordinary cases.

Owing to the short period of our stay in the country; our continual moving, seldom remaining twenty-four hours in the same place; the gross ignorance of the people in general; and our imperfect knowledge of their language, which prevented a free communication with the few well-informed persons we were so fortunate as to meet with—it was extremely difficult to obtain accurate information upon any subject. It is therefore by no means improbable that I may have been led into error occasionally in my remarks on the manners and customs of the Spaniards, or in the description of the places we visited; but I noted everything as it appeared to me at the time, and if there be mistakes in these pages, I trust they are neither numerous nor important.

A. G.

THE JOURNAL OF
A CAVALRY OFFICER IN THE
CORUNNA CAMPAIGN

CHAPTER I

[*THE campaign of Vimiera was over; the French,
hitherto invincible upon the Continent of Europe,
had felt in the Peninsula the weight of the British
arms, and had been no less surprised than demoral-
ized. The agreement known as the Convention of
Cintra—but which had been negotiated near Torres
Vedras and signed at Lisbon—had been completed :
Portugal was set free and its harbours secured
as the base for future operations. The three British
Generals—Sir Hew Dalrymple, Sir Harry Burrard,
and Sir Arthur Wellesley—who had put their names
to the Convention and to the armistice which had
preceded it, had gone to England to answer for
their actions before a court of inquiry, leaving in
command of the British army in Portugal Sir John
Moore, who had landed at Lisbon while the arrange-*

1

ments for the conclusion of the Convention were in progress.

Shortly before the British forces had arrived in the country, the Spaniards had defeated the French under Dupont at Baylen, when the whole population at once sprang to arms. The French army hurriedly retired behind the River Ebro, and the Spanish forces now reoccupied Madrid, and pushed forward three armies—in Biscay, beyond Tudela, and into Aragon —to oppose the French, to drive them from Spain, and even, as some boasted, to pursue them across the Pyrenees. So soon as the news of Dupont's disaster reached Napoleon, he sent off reinforcements, and an amended scheme of operations to deal with the situation which had arisen; and finally, on October 30, 1808, he left Paris to take command in person of the army of 250,000 men now gathered in the Peninsula.

On October 6 despatches from England had reached Sir John Moore at Lisbon, informing him of his appointment to the chief command of the army to be employed in Spain—an army which, with a force still to sail from Falmouth to Corunna, would comprise some 40,000 men. Sir John Moore's natural exultation at his good fortune finds expression in his diary, wherein, under date of October 14, he writes: "There has been no such command since Marlborough for a British officer."

*The original object with which the British ex-
peditionary force had been sent to the Peninsula—
the expulsion of the French from Portugal—had
been achieved by Wellesley's victories and by the
fulfilment of the terms of the Convention of Cintra;
but there had been considerable uncertainty among
the Ministers at home as to the direction which any
future operations should take, and while Dalrymple
was in chief command he had been asked to forward
suggestions as to where and in what manner an
army of 30,000 or 40,000 men could most profit-
ably be employed. Two plans finally assumed
prominence: either that the British should advance
across the frontiers of Portugal into Spain, and,
in combination with the Spanish forces, attack the
French immediately in their front; or that they
should re-embark, proceed to Asturias by sea, and
assail the French armies in flank and rear. Finally,
on September 25, it had been decided that the whole
of the British army then in Portugal should act
in co-operation with the Spanish forces in the North
of Spain for the expulsion of the French; and it was
left to Moore, when the command of the British
army was ultimately confided to him, either to
embark his troops and go to Corunna by sea, or
to march them by land from Lisbon to Valladolid,
where he hoped to effect the junction of all his forces
He decided to move by land for the reasons given in*

his diary—viz., that " the passage by sea is pre-carious, an embarkation unhinges, and when I get to Corunna I should still have to equip the army before I could stir, and in Galicia it might have been impossible to have found sufficient means of carriage."

But it is important to note, for it is a point which critics of Moore's operations are apt sometimes to overlook, that, in the instructions communicated at various times both to Moore himself and to his pre-decessors in command, it seems clear that the British force—not only a British army, but the only one England then possessed—was entrusted to him for the purpose of co-operating as an auxiliary body with formed and organized Spanish forces in the field ; that these forces were believed to be not less than 100,000 strong; that the armies of France then operating in Spain were estimated at scarcely more than half that strength ; while the British force could scarcely effect its concentration covered by the Spanish armies strung out, under a number of more or less independent commanders, along a front of 200 miles.

Having decided to move forward by road, Sir John Moore, mindful that the rainy season was at hand, had now to determine what route or routes he should follow. Certain inquiries as to the general condition of the roads had been set on foot by

Dalrymple, who had, however, done little in the direction of collecting transport or supplies. The local authorities could give Moore but small information as to whether any or which of the roads were practicable for the passage of artillery; but the general consensus of opinion seemed to be that all the roads north of the Tagus were impassable by guns. Moore finally decided to move by four roads, and on October 11 his leading regiments started from Lisbon on the march which was to end at Corunna, and cover the army with " glory, disgrace, victory, and misfortune."

The following, then, were the routes taken from Lisbon and Elvas to Salamanca, and the troops that traversed them :

*By Coimbra and Celorico : Beresford's Brigade—
    1st Battalion 9th, 2nd Battalion 43rd, and
    2nd Battalion 52nd.*

    Fane's Brigade—1st Battalion 38th, 1st Battalion 79th, and four companies 2nd Battalion 95th.

*By Abrantes and Guarda : Bentinck's Brigade
    —1st Battalion 4th, 1st Battalion 28th, 1st Battalion 42nd, and four companies 2nd Battalion 95th.*

    Hill's Brigade—1st Battalion 5th, 1st Battalion 32nd, and 1st Battalion 91st.

2

By Elvas and Alcantara: Anstruther's Brigade—
  20th, 1st Battalion 52nd, and five companies
  1st Battalion 95th.
  Alten's Brigade—1st and 2nd Light Infantry
  of the King's German Legion.

Five companies 5th Battalion 60th also accompanied Moore's force.

One battery of artillery accompanied the Abrantes and Guarda column.

It was confidently asserted, by those who seemed to Moore best qualified to know, that none of the above three roads were fit for the passage of guns, and he therefore decided, much against his better judgment, that his artillery must follow a fourth road, which led south of the Tagus by Elvas and Badajoz, crossed the Tagus at Almaraz, and thence proceeded by Talavera, the Escurial Pass, Espinar, and Arevalo. By this route marched the remaining six batteries with the army, the 18th Hussars, the 3rd Light Dragoons of the King's German Legion, and the 2nd, 36th, five companies of the 5th Battalion 60th, 71st, and 92nd Regiments, the whole under Sir John Hope. By this arrangement, which seems under the circumstances to have been all but unavoidable, the junction of the British forces was considerably delayed; while Hope's column, moreover, had to move in somewhat dangerous proximity to the enemy. This risk was not diminished by the fact that, owing to want of money and supplies, bad transport, and losses among his horses, Hope had to move his column in six small parties, each one day's march in rear of the other.

Having seen nearly all his troops out of Lisbon, Moore started himself from that city on October 27, leaving behind him a division of British troops for the protection of the capital, Elvas, and Almeida, under Sir John Cradock, who had been sent out from home, and whose arrival in Portugal was then hourly expected. This division numbered some 9,000 men, and was made up of the 3rd Buffs, then garrisoning Almeida, the 1st Battalion 6th, 9th, 29th, 40th, 45th, 50th, 82nd, and 97th Regiments, the remnants of the 20th Light Dragoons, and six batteries of artillery. The 3rd and 50th were to follow Moore when relieved by the 3rd Battalion 27th and 2nd Battalion 31st, which regiments had left England with Baird, while the 1st Battalion 6th and 82nd also later joined the main army, but the Buffs were sent back to Portugal from Salamanca.

In the meantime the home authorities had been busied in the preparation of the force to be sent from England to join Moore, which was to consist of nearly 14,000 of all ranks, and to be commanded by Sir David Baird. In September Sir David proceeded to Cork to superintend the embarkation of his troops, and was then told not to wait for the horses for his batteries, which would be sent after him; he very properly, however, refused to start without them.   From Cork the transports sailed to, and were concentrated at, Falmouth, which port was left on October 8, the fleet eventually reaching Corunna on the 13th.   Baird's force was thus composed:

1st and 3rd Battalions 1st Guards, 3rd Battalion 1st, 2nd Battalion 14th, 2nd Battalion 23rd, 1st Battalion 26th, 1st Battalion 43rd, 51st, 2nd Battalion 59th, 76th, 2nd Battalion 81st, five companies 1st Battalion 95th, six companies 2nd Battalion 95th.

With Baird there also sailed three field batteries, but the arm in which Moore was weakest was cavalry, and the three reinforcing regiments of this arm— 7th, 10th, and 15th Hussars—were by some mismanagement at home shipped off last of all.]

The Fifteenth or King's Regiment of Light Dragoons (Hussars), having received orders to prepare for foreign service, marched from Romford Barracks to Portsmouth, where our embarkation was completed on Sunday, October 30, 1808.

I went with part of my troop on board the *Rodney*, a ship of 300 tons burden, fitted up to receive forty men and thirty-six horses. Major Leitch, Surgeon Lidderdale, and Cornet Phillips (who had just joined the regiment from Eton), took their passage in the same vessel; and, with the exception of the Major, who occupied the state cabin, we were wretchedly accommodated. The berths were so bad that Lidderdale and myself preferred sleeping in cots slung in the cabin to the risk of being poisoned by the smell of the bilge-water, and a bed was prepared on the floor for Phillips. As soon as the horses were got on board, the master of the *Rodney* went to take his amusement in the town; and, as he did not make his appearance late in the afternoon of the next day—long after orders had been given for the transports to quit the harbour —I went on shore to make a complaint to the Commissioner of Transports, who promised to appoint another to the command. About three o'clock, however, our friend returned in a state of intoxication, and we proceeded to our station in Stokes Bay, where we were terribly tossed all night, and most of our glass and crockery was broken.

On November 2 the fleet, consisting of thirty-five sail of transports, left Stokes Bay under convoy of the *Endymion* frigate, commanded by the Hon. Captain Capel.

It was a fine autumnal evening, and the moon, which had risen in full splendour before we cleared the Solent, shed its mild radiance on the landscape, and enabled us to trace each well-known spot in the beautiful scenery of the Isle of Wight and opposite coast. Notwithstanding the exultation with which we had hailed the signal for "getting under weigh," I could not banish the melancholy idea that we were quitting our friends and our country perhaps to return to them no more ; and, whilst watching the track of the vessel until it was lost in the surrounding waters, I reflected that in a few short weeks my own career might be closed, and all traces of my existence equally obliterated. I was roused from this gloomy reverie by the cries of a poor boy, who had been washed out of a boat at the stern of one of the transports, nearly abreast of the *Rodney*. Owing to the rate at which we were sailing, all attempts to rescue him were ineffectual, and his cries became fainter and fainter until we could hear them no longer. His only chance of escape rested on his being noticed by some of the sternmost ships, but in all probability he perished.

The breeze freshened soon after we passed the Needles, and I was driven below by a violent attack of sea-sickness, and I suffered so much from this malady during the whole voyage that I could seldom venture to leave my cot, or even to sit up in it. Seven or eight sail parted from the convoy during the night, and we pursued our course with favourable weather until Sunday, the 6th, when we encountered a squall, which damaged some of the transports. Our ship rolled so excessively that we every moment expected her masts to go overboard. Several of the horses were thrown down—the labouring of the vessel having displaced some of the bars which divided the stalls—and one of them was so much injured that we were obliged to destroy him.

We also lost a fine piece of fresh beef, which was dislodged from its place in the maintop, and, besides occasioning considerable alarm below-deck by the crash, nearly demolished the Major in its descent!

We were at this time in the Bay of Biscay,

and I was struck with astonishment at the
prodigious swell after the gale had subsided ;
the waves were so immense that, when our
vessel was in the trough of the sea, we could not
discern the masthead of a single ship of the fleet,
although some of them were almost within
hail.　On the 7th the convoy was thrown into
some alarm by the appearance of a French
privateer, to which the *Endymion* gave chase,
and soon quieted our apprehensions.

At daybreak on the 8th there was a thick
fog, which cleared away about nine o'clock, and
we found ourselves close in with the land under
Cape Ortegal.　We immediately stood off, and
anchored in the Bay of Corunna the same evening.
About half an hour before the fog cleared away,
I inquired of the master of the *Rodney* " when
he expected to get into port " ?　Upon which he
asserted that we were above a hundred miles
from land, so that, if the haze had not dispersed
thus opportunely, in all probability we should
have been wrecked, as the ship was going at the
rate of six or seven knots an hour with her head
right to the breakers.

The Bay of Corunna was crowded with
shipping ; and the fleet, with the 7th and 10th

Light Dragoons (Hussars) and two troops of Horse Artillery on board, which left Yarmouth Roads (Isle of Wight) two days before we sailed, arrived about the same time we did. As it was quite dark before the heavy sailers reached their stations, some of them ran foul of those already at anchor, notwithstanding the numerous lights displayed ; and for some hours there was an incessant uproar and confusion occasioned by the squabbles betwixt the crews of vessels which came in contact or *athwart hawse.*

In the course of the night the wind freshened, and it blew a hard gale in the morning. The *Rodney* was anchored above a mile from the quay, and it was with difficulty I could prevail upon the master to set me on shore ; but I had suffered so dreadfully from sea-sickness, and found myself so much reduced by it, that I was determined not to remain on board a single hour after it was practicable to quit the ship. The weather becoming more moderate about noon, Major Leitch and myself got into the boat, which was nearly swamped before we could get clear of the vessel, and rowed to the harbour. We had scarcely landed before we had a sample of the violence of the rains in Spain at this season of the year; a shower poured down like a waterspout, and soaked us to the skin before we could find shelter. The town was crowded with the officers and men of Sir David Baird's army, which had disembarked a few days before our arrival; and it was fortunate for us that several divisions had already moved to the interior of the country, as we should otherwise have been obliged to remain on board our transports. Even as it was, I traversed the streets for a considerable time without any prospect of procuring either food or lodging. At the Leon d'Oro, the principal hotel in the place, I could obtain nothing but a glass of liqueur and a few apples. At length, happening to meet Captain McMahon of the 60th Regiment, who had formerly served in the 15th, he conducted me to the Hotel d'Ingleterra — which we afterwards called the "British"—where a *table d'hôte* was established, and the landlord, an Italian, who could speak French a little, promised, as a particular favour, to accommodate me with an apartment in his house.

At four o'clock we repaired to the dining-room, where about thirty persons, chiefly British officers, were assembled. The tablecloth was coarse and

dirty ; the forks and spoons, which were silver,
looked like pewter ; the salt was coarse, brown,
and almost tasteless ; and the apparatus of the
table was completed by a mixture of pepper, oil,
and vinegar, which was called "mustard," although
not a particle of that seed had been used in its
composition. A decanter filled with a weak red
wine, the growth of the province, was placed
beside each cover ; it is the ordinary beverage,
plain or diluted, but I do not think those
who drink it unmixed run the smallest risk of
intoxication. Malt liquor is rarely to be met
with.

After waiting a considerable time, the company, who were all pretty sharp-set, began to
show signs of impatience at the delay of their
dinner, which at length made its appearance,
served by our host and two or three ill-looking
fellows, each with a dirty napkin thrown *grace-
fully* over the left shoulder. The repast consisted of a profusion of meat, game, fish, and
poultry, with a dessert, and as much of the
execrable *vino-tinto* as we chose to drink, for
which each person paid sixteen reals—about three
shillings and fourpence.

The scene during dinner was highly diverting ;

the awkward attempts of some of the party to speak French or Spanish were truly ridiculous, whilst others called for what they wanted in English, and seemed quite astonished at not being understood by the wondering waiters, whom they damned for stupid scoundrels. A trait of the national character was displayed in the conduct of these ragamuffins, who attended with alacrity to the call of those who addressed them by the title of *señor*, whilst they took as little notice as possible of those who vociferated *muchacho!*

I went to the theatre in the evening, and on my return to the hotel was ushered to my bedroom, which certainly had no very inviting appearance. It was a small cockloft about 10 feet square ; the scanty portion of light that was admitted came through a pane of coarse green glass, fixed in a sort of wooden chimney in the middle of the ceiling, and there was no mode of obtaining fresh air except by keeping the door open. The furniture consisted of a chair, a table, and a pallet with a hard mattress. By dint of earnest entreaties, I procured the addition of a basin and towel, which the people of the house seemed to consider as quite an unreasonable indulgence. The basins used in this country are either large and shallow, like a pie-dish, or round and deep; but they invariably have a broad rim with a notch in it, and bear a sufficient resemblance to the skullcaps, formerly worn, to warrant Don Quixote's mistake in the affair of Mambrino's helmet. The materials are generally silver, copper, or brass, although they are sometimes made of earthenware. The sheets and pillow-cases were of very fine linen, and edged with a broad frill of muslin or cambric, which did not correspond with the mean appearance of the bedstead and furniture.

I slept very comfortably in this wretched garret—infinitely preferable, in my opinion, to the best accommodation of a transport—but was glad to exchange it for a less elevated apartment which became vacant in a day or two.

In consequence of the place not affording stable room for so large a body of cavalry, a part of our brigade was obliged to remain on board the ships until the departure of the troops which were first landed; and the Fifteenth was not disembarked for some days. This delay proved very detrimental to the horses, and they fell off

3

rapidly in point of condition ; many of them lost the use of their legs for a time, and some were rendered quite unserviceable.

The *Nelson*, our headquarters ship, having Colonel Grant, Captain Murray, the Paymaster, and the Adjutant, on board, was one of the vessels which had separated from the convoy, and for several days we entertained considerable apprehensions on their account. At length, however, after giving up all hopes of them, we had the satisfaction to see her enter the harbour. We also received information that two of the transports which were missing had put into Muros Bay. One of them, which carried Cornet Jenkins and about thirty hussars, had been taken by a French privateer ; but a British sloop of war coming in sight obliged the enemy to abandon their prize before they had time to shift the prisoners or to destroy the horses. The Commander, however, took away all the arms he could discover, and obliged the officer to give his parole not to serve against France or her allies during the war. The validity of this convention was disallowed at headquarters, notwithstanding the urgent remonstrances of poor Jenkins, who was afraid of being shot for break-

ing his parole, if he should have the misfortune
to be taken prisoner a second time.

The last division of the infantry left Corunna
on November 10; one regiment and a battalion
of detachments remained to guard the ammunition and military stores, and to garrison the
citadel. Sir David Baird with his staff followed
in a day or two, and on the 15th three troops of
the 7th Hussars, forming the first division of the
cavalry, commenced their march. The difficulty
of procuring forage, and the want of accommodation for the horses in the miserable villages of
Galicia, obliged us to move in small detachments; and in order to spare the horses as much
as possible, and allow them time to recover from
the effects of confinement during the voyage,
the route to Astorga was divided into twelve
easy stages with two halting days.

Having no military duties to attend to during
the interval between our arrival and the disem-
barkation of the regiment, I employed that period
in visiting everything worthy of notice in the
town; but as my horses were still on shipboard
I was prevented from making any excursions
into the adjacent country, and thus lost the
opportunity of seeing Ferrol, which I particu-

larly regretted, as it is reckoned the chief naval arsenal of Spain, and is one of the largest and most complete establishments of the kind in the world.

Corunna is situated on a peninsula at the end of a fine bay, sheltered by hills which rise immediately behind the town. The harbour is excellent, and capable of containing a numerous fleet; it is in the form of a crescent, and the entrance is defended by the Castle of St. Antonio, built on a steep rock which commands the roadstead. This castle is also used as a State prison. The harbour is, besides, protected by three forts and by the citadel, which is a tolerably regular fortification, but in a neglected state, and incapable of defence against an attack from the land side, as it is commanded by the surrounding hills, and the lower town extends nearly to the foot of the glacis. The citadel is situated on a rocky promontory, and encloses the new town of Corunna within its walls. The streets are narrow and ill-paved; the houses are lofty, but have little architectural beauty to recommend them, although the hotels of the principal nobility of the province are to be found there. The theatre stands in the fosse which has been excavated from the solid rock.

Upon a hill near the citadel stands an ancient tower of considerable strength and elevation ; the erection of this building is attributed by the Galicians to Hercules, whose name it bears. It is also called the Iron Tower, and is undoubtedly of very great antiquity, although historians are divided in opinion whether it is a Phœnician or a Roman work. Whatever its origin, the building is now converted into a lighthouse—which is probably the use for which it was first designed —and is, from its situation, a conspicuous landmark to vessels at sea. The Iron Tower forms the armorial bearings of the town of Corunna.

There were no regular Spanish troops in garrison here ; but I saw about 600 Patriots, who mounted guards and shared fatigue duties with our infantry. These volunteers were wretchedly clothed and but indifferently armed, and their appearance was by no means calculated to impress an observer with a very high opinion of their prowess ; but I was at this time sanguine in the cause, and persuaded myself that these peasants possessed an invincible courage, which would counterbalance every other deficiency. I understood that 5,000 volunteers had been equipped at this place, and sent to join General

4

Blake's army; and that recruits were continually forwarded to his headquarters as fast as they could be supplied with arms, and drilled to the manual and platoon exercises.

In addition to these disposable levies, a number of the principal inhabitants had formed themselves into a corps for the defence of the town; and although their enrolment was but of recent date, they made a very respectable appearance.

The lower town, called also Pescaderia, or fishmarket, which extends almost to the walls of the citadel, occupies a narrow neck of land formed by the harbour on one side, and Orsan Bay on the other. At the opposite extremity a line of entrenchments is carried across the isthmus, and, at the distance of a quarter of a mile, the suburb of St. Lucia stretches along the harbour. This suburb is a place of some extent, and contains large barracks, as well as magazines of naval and military stores. The aqueduct, which supplies the town with water from the neighbouring hills, is also to be seen in this direction. Corunna, including St. Lucia, extends about two miles along the bay, and, according to the best information I could procure, contains nearly 6,000 inhabitants. There are four parish churches, four convents, and two hospitals, in the citadel and lower town; there are three squares with a fountain in each; but none of the buildings, either public or private, have been erected with any view to external ornament—even the churches are only remarkable for the plainness and solidity of their structure. The streets are steep and narrow, extremely dirty, and paved with large flat stones, upon which our horses could with difficulty keep their footing.

The merchants and shopkeepers reside in the lower town, where all the business and commerce of the place is transacted. There are some extensive hat manufactories, and the chocolate made here is highly esteemed; the shops are numerous, but the greater part of the articles on sale—which are chiefly of foreign manufacture—are highly priced and of inferior quality. The hotels are very indifferent, and the conduct of many of the landlords was quite unaccountable; upon the first arrival of the British troops they were perfectly willing to accommodate small parties of officers with board and lodging, but when the number of customers increased they either shut up their houses or restricted their business to the furnishing of coffee, chocolate,

etc., and we could not prevail upon them to provide us with a dinner on any terms.   The motives
for this behaviour, so evidently at variance with
their interest, always remained a mystery to us.
The only description of cart used in this province
is a miserable vehicle, the body of which is composed of a few rough planks, tied or nailed
together, to form the bottom, with three or four
stakes placed upright on each side at intervals of
two feet.   From the front of the platform issues
a pole, to the ends of which the oxen are harnessed
by the horns, instead of being yoked by the neck,
as is usual in other countries.   The wheels are
solid, and do not revolve on the axletree, but the
axle itself turns round, making the most horrible
creaking that can be imagined.   The Spaniards,
although they make such liberal use of grease
in their kitchens, seem most scrupulously to
refrain from applying the smallest portion to the
wheels of these infernal machines.   The concert
formed by a train of these cars, accompanied by
the cries of the drivers to encourage their cattle,
is almost sufficient to make anyone within reach
of the sounds pray to be divested of the sense of
hearing.

Southey, in his " Travels in Spain," speaking

of the cars used in Galicia, mentions that the Governor of Corunna once ordered them to be kept well oiled to prevent the horrid creaking of the wheels. But the drivers petitioned against it, declaring that the oxen liked the sound and would not draw without it. The order was revoked in consequence. Another reason alleged by them is that the noise frightens away the devil, who would otherwise injure the animals. It is said—with greater probability—to have the effect of scaring the wolves, which might certainly do mischief to the oxen in the wild mountainous districts, if they were not kept off by this frightful sound.

The few coaches and chariots I saw in this part of the country are exceedingly heavy and old-fashioned; they appear to have been built on the model of the carriages represented in the plates which embellish the old editions of "Don Quixote" and "Gil Blas." The harness is commonly composed of ropes, but the carriage mules are frequently very superb. Those which I saw, belonging to the Duke of Veragua, measured about sixteen hands in height, and cost 300 dollars each. Litters are sometimes used in making journeys or transporting the sick; the body is that of a coach, chariot, or sedan-chair, fixed, like the latter, upon poles and carried betwixt the mules.

The houses of the hidalgos are spacious, but meanly fitted up and ill-furnished—in fact, an English tradesman lives more comfortably, and in some respects even more luxuriously, than a grandee of Spain. Whilst I remained at Corunna I had the honour of dining with the Duke of Veragua, a grandee of the first class, and one of the knights of Calatrava. He is the lineal descendant, by the female line, and representative of the discoverer of America, who is called Colon by the Spaniards. The palace of Veragua stands in the citadel, and is by far the most comfortable house to which I had access during our short abode in the country. It is furnished pretty much in the English style, and some of the apartments are fitted up with an attention to convenience and comfort which is seldom found out of Britain. I was much disappointed with a portrait of Columbus which hangs in one of the antechambers. I expected to have seen a countenance indicative of profound thought and gentle disposition combined with resolution, but the face produced by the painter is compounded of vulgarity and stupidity. In one corner of the canvas the armorial bearings of the family are emblazoned with the arms of Castile and Leon in an escutcheon of pretence. The crest is a ship circumnavigating the globe, with the following Spanish couplet by way of motto :

" A la Castilla y a Leon,
Nuevo Mondo dio Colon."

The present Duke does not appear to have inherited either the abilities or the energy of mind of his illustrious progenitor, but he is affable, cheerful, and hospitable. He pressed me very much to take up my abode in his house during the remainder of my stay at Corunna, and offered me the apartment Mr. Stuart had occupied a few weeks before. I was obliged to decline this civility, which would have been attended with a great deal of inconvenience, but was much indebted to him for the use of an excellent stable for my horses, which had been very ill-accommodated in that respect before. When I dined with the Duke, the party consisted of six Spaniards, one of whom was a naval officer, and two of the others had the look of secular priests. The Duchess was at a country-seat at

some distance. I regretted her absence, as I
wished for an opportunity of observing the
manners of a Spanish lady of high rank. I was
told that she was very handsome and very agreeable, and that her husband was so jealous that
he had retired from the Court some months ago,
in order to withdraw her from the too particular
attentions of one of the French officers. The
Duke and two of his friends understood French,
but had great difficulty in expressing themselves
in that language. The conversation, of course,
was carried on chiefly in Spanish, in which I had
made but little progress, and therefore could not
enter much into the subjects of discourse, which
generally turned upon the situation of public
affairs, and it appeared to me that the expectations of the majority were not very sanguine.

We dined at three o'clock, and were served
on plate which would have looked splendid if it
had been properly cleaned ; but, from the slovenly
manner in which it is kept, plate does not give
the same éclat to an entertainment in Spain that
it does in England.

The first course consisted of soups and roast
meat, followed by fish and boiled meat ; then a
course of poultry and game ; and lastly pastry

and confections, in which the Spanish cooks excel. Each person carved the dish that happened to be next him by cutting portions of it into a plate, which was then handed round the table for the company to help themselves. By this means, as the plates followed each other in quick succession, and it seemed to be the rule to refuse nothing, we had several different kinds of food before us at the same time. Of the domestics who waited upon us—six or seven in number—only two were in livery, one was in the habit of a page, and the rest were dressed in very shabby suits. The butler wore a threadbare coat with one of the sleeves nearly torn off, and was more occupied in endeavouring to conceal this misfortune than in attending to his duty at the sideboard. He appeared, however, to be exceedingly amused by the conversation, and laughed heartily at his master's jokes, throwing in a few remarks of his own occasionally.

I happened to meet him in the street next day, when he accosted me with the greatest familiarity and offered to shake hands, a freedom which rather astonished me ; but when I became better acquainted with the manners of the people, I observed that it was customary for servants to take such kind of liberties, and that they were always on the most familiar footing with their employers. The nobility generally retain the servants of their deceased relations, and a domestic is seldom discarded except for some heinous offence, or from incapacity for service, in which case he is allowed a pension. This system must occasion an enormous expense to the grandees, many of whom have several dozen idle retainers to provide for.

The wine we drank at dinner was the common *vin du pays*, scarcely superior in quality to that furnished at the *table d'hôte*. The Duke and his friends took large draughts of it, and seemed to relish it prodigiously. I have often heard the Galicians expatiate on its virtues, and many of our soldiers drank it to excess, although I can only compare the taste of it to a mixture of vinegar and ink. In general it is so weak that one would scarcely believe it possible to drink sufficient to cause intoxication; but when mulled with plenty of sugar and spice it is not unpalatable. The dinner was followed by an elegant dessert, when the *vino tinto* was replaced by three or four sorts of rich sweet wines, of which we drank a few glasses, and then adjourned to

the drawing room, where coffee was served, soon
after which I withdrew, and the Spaniards went
to take their siesta.

Many of the principal families which usually
reside in Corunna were absent while we were in
the place, but soon after our arrival a grand ball
was given to the officers by a Countess whose
name I do not recollect. The company was
numerous, and we danced minuets, waltzes, and
country-dances ; the entertainment was altogether so much in the English style that it
afforded no criterion by which we could form an
opinion of Spanish manners.

I occasionally spent the evening at *tertullas*,
which are private assemblies, or conversaziónes,
and always found these parties exceedingly dull ;
the company generally consisted of from ten to
twenty persons, the majority priests and friars, in
a spacious room scantily furnished and ill-lighted.
Cards, conversation, and music, formed the
agrémens of the evening ; sugared biscuits and
lemonade were sometimes offered, but this ceremony was more frequently dispensed with. The
gentlemen seldom appear at these parties without their cigars, which are often passed from
mouth to mouth in long succession, and both

sexes have an abominable habit of spitting on the floors.

In the houses of the merchants and poor hidalgos it is customary to have a bed in the parlour or family sitting-room, placed within an alcove, and the apartment is equally used by the inmates, whether the occupier of the bed is in it or not, without appearing to make the slightest embarrassment on either side. The females in the houses where we were billeted often visited us in the morning before we got up, to ask us how we had passed the night and to bring us our chocolate ; they then entered into conversation, and sometimes extended their visits to such a length that we were obliged to request them to retire.

The costume of the nation varies so much in the different provinces and stations of life that it is difficult to give a general description of it. Dark colours are commonly worn by the men, who, when they go abroad, are always muffled up in the *capa*, a long and ample cloak, which effectually conceals the face as well as the person, and gives to each individual the appearance of a bravo. Black is the colour most esteemed for full dress, and, amongst the peasantry, distinguishes the master of the family from his servants. In several districts they wear slouch hats with very broad brims, which must be of essential utility in a country where the rays of the sun are so powerful. But in Galicia and the northern parts of Leon the *montero* cap is commonly worn; it is very convenient, and at the same time picturesque. The peasants frequently go bare-legged, and wooden shoes are much used by both sexes.

The French mode of dress is pretty generally adopted by the ladies, but many still adhere to the ancient Spanish costume, which is so becoming that it is much to be regretted it should have given place to any other. This habit consists of a body and petticoat of silk or satin, trimmed with velvet, over which is worn a dress of lace, terminated by a fringe of silken cords, which reaches to the knees. The mantilla, a lace veil or scarf, which covers the head and falls over the neck and shoulders, is worn with this dress, instead of a hat or bonnet. This elegant habit, which is always worn at Mass, is on those occasions invariably black—indeed, it is rare to see it in colours. The women wear short petticoats in order to display their feet and ankles, which are well proportioned ; they step well, pay particular attention to their *chaussure*, and their air in walking is remarkably graceful. Cocked hats are universally worn by the gentry and middling classes, and even by boys of seven or eight years old, who also wear long coats and boots. It is by no means unusual to see children who can scarcely walk, dressed like grown-up women in short petticoats, bodice, and scarf, looking as old-fashioned as if they were grandmothers. This early imitation of the dress of their elders gives the very infants a most grave and sedate appearance ; and the formal behaviour and pompous manner of children under eight years of age is highly ludicrous.

The theatre, usually called the " opera," is the only place of public amusement at Coruhna. It is larger than most of the provincial theatres in Britain, and greater attention is paid to the accommodation of the public. The benches in the pit have backs and each seat is numbered, and the tickets of admission are numbered to correspond, so that every person's place is marked by his ticket. All crowding and disputes for places are by these means avoided, and it is easy to secure any particular seat by applying in the morning for the number desired. Females never appear in the pit—indeed, I believe there is a regulation to prevent them. The scenery and decorations are tolerably good, the music very indifferent. The performances consist of comedies and stories from sacred history; among those I saw represented were Daniel in the Den of Lions; Susannah and the Elders; Shadrach, Meshach, and Abednego, in the Fiery Furnace; Nebuchadnezzar's Metamorphosis. These representations were truly absurd, and only calculated to turn the subject into ridicule, which certainly was not the intention either of the author or the actors.

Men in tawdry dresses performed the part of the lions, who rolled about the stage like blind puppies, and "aggravated their voices" like Bottom, so that they "roar'd as gently as any sucking doves." Allegorical pieces in allusion to the situation of the country were often performed, in which Spain, under the figure of a beautiful woman, was represented as enslaved by the treachery of France, and liberated by the exertions of England. On these occasions our venerable Monarch, with several members of the Royal Family, were introduced upon the stage

to embrace Ferdinand, and the spectacle concluded with the engagement of the latter to
marry an English Princess—the curtain falling
amidst shouts of "Viva Fernando !" "Viva
Gorge tercero !" "Viva Spana !" "Viva Ingleterra !"

The prompter's head appears from a little box
just above the boards in front of the stage, and
he reads every speech from beginning to end
with as loud a voice as the actors' recite. They
declaim in a querulous tone, and do not use
much gesture. The principal actress was blind
of one eye—a blemish which I observed not
infrequently amongst the women. The dancing
was the only part of the performance which
excited much interest, and the ballets generally
concluded with the fandango or the bolero,
danced by persons habited in the costume of
Andalusia. The two principal dancers would
not have disgraced our opera, and the effect of
the castanets added much to the spirit of the
scene.

During the time I remained at Corunna I
made some progress in learning the language,
and neglected no opportunity of speaking it.
I soon understood Spanish sufficiently to read

the public journals, which teemed with abuse of
the Bonaparte family ; and the chief efforts of the
editor's ingenuity seemed to be employed in the
invention of nicknames. Napoleon was converted by the patriots into " Napo-ladron." If
we happened to mention the name of Bonaparte,
we were immediately interrupted, and desired to
say " Malaparte." Joseph, their new King, has
obtained the reputation of being immoderately
addicted to the bottle ; and, as the people look
upon a drunkard with contempt and abhorrence,
they have been particularly severe in the epithets
they have applied to him—Josef-boracho, Rey
de botillas, Pepecubas, etc., are appellations
very liberally bestowed upon him by all who
profess attachment to Ferdinand. But it would
appear that they suffer their zeal in his cause to
evaporate in abuse of the usurper of his throne,
for I never saw any disposition in his partisans
to incur the slightest personal risk in his service.
Although our army marched above 800 miles
in the country, it was not joined by a single
Spaniard ; and even where the spirit of patriotism
appeared to be in its zenith, the people seemed
to think they gave ample support to the good
cause by hailing us with *vivas* as we passed, and

6

by furnishing us with provisions for which we paid the full value.

From the character given of Ferdinand by his friends, I should imagine that he is totally unfit to wield a sceptre; the only reply I ever obtained to my inquiries respecting his abilities— from those who professed themselves his most devoted adherents—was that he was " mucho pio." Now, although this character—which must be understood to mean that he is a bigot to the superstitions of the Church of Rome—would be a suitable recommendation to an abbacy or a bishopric, I question whether it will enable him to govern an extensive empire with advantage to his subjects if he should ever recover the throne, which at present seems rather problematical.

CHAPTER II

[Much had happened between the departure from
England of the advanced portion of Baird's force,
and the eastward move from Corunna of his cavalry
brigade. The troops which sailed with Sir David
reached their destination on October 13, but were not
permitted by the Spanish authorities to land until the
26th, being then pushed forward into Leon in small
parties. By November 4 all these had been put on
shore, and, so soon as he had seen the arrival of the last
of the transports conveying his mounted troops, Sir
David Baird started to join his infantry at Astorga.
On the road, Baird heard of the ill-fate which had
pursued the Spanish armies—Blake's reverse at
Zornosa, Belvedere's route at Gamonal, Blake's over-
throw at Espinosa, the crushing of Castanos. He
must have learnt during his halt at Astorga that
Asturias lay at the feet of the French, who were
already in Valladolid, with their cavalry at Benevente on the road to Salamanca, where Baird was
to have joined hands with Moore. Baird now saw
no course open to him but to retreat.

*Meanwhile Moore had reached Salamanca on
November 13, also met at every halting-place by
tidings of French successes, and he recognized that,
while he might gather his own troops round him at
Salamanca, a junction with those under Baird was
impossible should the French continue to advance.
On the 21st Moore bid Baird prepare for retreat ;
on the 23rd Moore's infantry had all joined him, but
on the 28th came news of the disaster at Tudela, and
Moore then decided himself to retreat on Portugal,
directed Baird to fall back on Corunna, embarking
thence for the Tagus, and ordered Hope to join at
once by forced marches.*

*Hope, by equal skill and good fortune, evaded
interference by the French, and was in touch with
Moore by December 4, by which date the situation
had already begun to show signs of improvement.
Napoleon, ceasing to move westward, was concentrating upon Madrid ; Blake's scattered army was being
reorganized ; the people of Madrid had flown to
arms, and were bent upon resistance. Moore felt
that he was in duty and in honour bound to support
the national movement, and cancelled the orders for
retreat, already in course of being carried out, and
on December 6 and 8 he directed Baird to send his
cavalry at once to Zamora, moving the remainder
of his force to Benevente.]*

The Cavalry and Horse Artillery marched in ten divisions ; the 15th Hussars formed the eighth and ninth ; and the last was composed of men and horses belonging to the brigade, who had been unable to accompany their respective corps. When I left Corunna the inhabitants were in the greatest consternation and distress, occasioned by accounts, which had arrived the evening before, of the destruction of General Blake's army in a series of actions near Reynosa.

November 23rd.—The tenth division, which did not exceed twenty-five men and horses, with Veterinary-Surgeon Castley, of the 15th, who was the only officer who accompanied me, was ordered to be in readiness to march at ten o'clock, but, owing to various causes of delay, we did not leave the barracks at St. Lucia until past twelve ; and as it was necessary to proceed slowly, on account of the weakly condition of the horses, it was four o'clock before we arrived at Betanzos, although the distance is little more than three leagues.

The road from Corunna to Astorga is perhaps one of the finest public works in Europe ; the country it passes through is in general mountainous, and the road is conducted along the side

of the hills, for the most part, about halfway
between the base and the summit; and in this
manner it is carried, by a very gradual ascent,
over some of the highest mountains in Galicia.
This road, which is broad and well formed, is
above 180 miles in length, and from the nature
of the ground, and the manner in which it is
executed, must have been a work of immense
expense and labour. The Spanish league measures
four English miles and about half a furlong; at
the end of each league a stone pillar is erected,
on which the distance from Corunna is marked.

The country between Corunna and Betanzos
is very beautiful; it is mountainous, but the
valleys are well cultivated, the hills verdant, and
occasionally clothed with wood. Betanzos is
finely situated in a bottom, completely surrounded by hills which offer many strong
positions. An arm of the sea runs nearly up
to the town, which stands on the banks of the
River Mandeo. But, notwithstanding the advantages of its situation, the place has very little
trade, and, from the dilapidated appearance of
many of the streets and houses, seems to be rapidly
falling into a state of complete decay. The town
is small, and contains no buildings worthy of

notice, with the exception of a large convent, which I had not leisure to enter.

The inhabitants appeared inclined to receive us with hospitality, but they were too indigent to show any substantial marks of their good-will. I was billeted at the house of a poor hidalgo, and accompanied my host and his lady to a *tertulla* at a house in the outskirts of the town. The whole assembly did not exceed eight persons; some of them played cards, and a young lady favoured us with a song which she accompanied by playing on the guitar, but I could not discover much melody either in the voice or the instrument. Having had no dinner, supper became an important consideration, and, observing no preparations for that meal, I retired to my quarters and regaled on hog's puddings and garlic *à l'Espagnole* with my host, who assured me he had entertained Admiral Cochrane at his house formerly.

24th.—As my instructions were to bring forward all the men and horses left on the road by the preceding divisions, the strength of the detachment augmented daily; and having been joined by a small party at Betanzos, we marched three leagues through a beautiful but very hilly

country, and halted for the night at Monte
Salgueiro. This *posada*,* a lone house situated
on an extensive heath, is one of the most miserable places I ever saw. The apartments we
occupied were filled with dirt, and the furniture
consisted of a clumsy deal table and form, and
two truckle bedsteads without blankets or bed-
ding of any kind. A Spanish family had arrived
just before us, and were dining, on some provisions they had brought with them, on a piazza in
front of the house, whilst the mules were baiting
in the courtyard. Their coach was filled with
blankets, pillows, and other articles which travel-
lers are obliged to carry with them, as the inns
in general only furnish house room and wine.

Even at this early period of the campaign, the
difficulty we experienced in procuring cars and
oxen for the conveyance of the baggage of the
army and military stores, might have satisfied us
of the little dependence to be placed on the co-
operation of the inhabitants. The peasants either
disregarded the orders of the *alcaldes* or obeyed
them with reluctance, and it was frequently
necessary to enforce obedience by threats and

* Monte Salgueiro was the name given to this inn by our
staff, but the proper name is Posada Castillana.

blows. The *alcaldes* themselves were in general but one degree above the lower class of peasants, who often treated them with disrespect ; on such occasions these village magistrates seemed to have no idea of keeping up the dignity of their office, nor any means of causing their authority to be regarded except the volubility of their tongues. Many of them were suspected of being well affected towards the enemy.

In many parts of this almost desert country wild - dogs prowl about in herds ; I saw the carcasses of two which had been shot the night before by some of our men, who were encamped on the moor. These animals resemble the wolf, but are smaller.

25th.—The weather had been remarkably fine for several days, but we marched this morning in a drizzling rain, which made our quarters appear even more wretched, and the thick mist which hung upon the mountains prevented us from seeing the country. At the end of two leagues we passed through a dirty, miserable-looking village called Gutoriez, and about a mile on the other side of it met Cornet Laroche, of the Fifteenth, who was proceeding with despatches to Corunna, and had orders to halt all the troops he should meet on the road, the intention of advancing being abandoned, as he told us, in consequence of the immense force the French were pouring into Castile, and the inefficient state of the Spanish armies.

In obedience to these orders, I returned with my detachment to Gutoriez, where I found a posada infinitely superior in point of accommodation to that at Monte Salgueiro. The land-lady, however, was a complete vixen, and the inhabitants of the village were so much irritated by the rumoured retreat of the British, that I expected them to give vent to their choler by attacking my small party. I therefore made arrangements for defending the house, which was a substantial stone building with a courtyard enclosed by a high wall; but fortunately the day passed without any unpleasant occurrence.

26*th*.—Received orders in the course of the morning to continue our advance, and marched two leagues to Bamondé, a pleasant little village situated in an extensive and fertile plain watered by the Mino, which is here a considerable river. The circumjacent country is well cultivated, and there are several detached farmhouses and *quintas* in the neighbourhood, which have a neat and comfortable appearance. Whilst taking a walk in the fields before dinner, I met a peasant carrying a hare he had just killed, which proved a very seasonable addition to our mess of tough ration beef. I gave the man a peseta (the fifth part of a dollar), which excited his gratitude to such a pitch that, before I was aware of his intentions, he threw his arms round my neck, and almost suffocated me with the stench of tobacco and garlic.

27th.—Marched to Lugo, four leagues. This city, once the metropolis of Spain, is of great antiquity, and was a Roman station under the name of Lucus Augusti. It is now the see of a Bishop, and is chiefly known on account of its warm medicinal springs. The ancient walls are of an extraordinary thickness, and still in good repair, and the town must have been a place of considerable strength from its commanding situation. It is supplied with water from the Mino by an aqueduct, and there is a handsome stone bridge across the river at the distance of half a league from the gates. The neighbouring country, which is broken into hill and dale, is very much intersected by dry stone walls, enclosing the fields and vineyards.

One quarter of the city is an open area, where
the foundations and ruins of buildings are very
apparent; in other respects Lugo, although
a gloomy and dirty place, does not exhibit the
marks of desertion and decay so evident in most
Spanish towns.   But I could not discover
whether this prosperity was owing to the profits
of trade, or merely to its being the seat of government for the province.   The cathedral is an
ancient Gothic edifice ; it has been repaired
lately, and the architect has added a portico in
the Grecian style, which spoils the effect of the
building.   The interior is very richly ornamented,
but there was not a great display of relics.

The city contains many churches and convents,
a college, and four hospitals ; the latter buildings
were converted into barracks and magazines, or
filled with the sick of our army, who were already
but too numerous.   The plaza, or great square,
is very spacious, the houses built on piazzas ;
there are several smaller squares, three of which
have fountains in the centre, covered with
grotesque decorations.   The population is com-
puted at 6,000 souls.   The episcopal palace is
a fine old building, but rather in a dilapidated
state.   The Bishop, who is about sixty years

of age, from his rotundity of person would not disgrace the English bench. He affected to adore the British, and expatiated in the most hyperbolical terms on the immense resources of the country and the energy of Spanish valour. I have since heard that he was secretly attached to the French party, which appears to have been the case from his subsequent conduct.

I received an invitation to dine with him, which I declined, but paid him a visit about noon, when I found him just beginning his meal, and was not a little edified by witnessing his abstinence! His figure recalled to my recollection the description given of the Canon Sedillo in " Gil Blas," except that he made good use of his hands. He was waited upon by a subaltern priest, who placed a single dish on the table, which he took care to remove as soon as the contents were devoured. The prelate dispensed with the use of either knife or fork, and contrived, with the assistance of two large bloodhounds, to empty near a dozen dishes of meat and pastry. Two priests conversed with him during his repast, and he again pressed me to dine with his family at three o'clock. He appeared to be a good-humoured, ignorant old man. I saw him

7

afterwards in the dusk of the evening taking an airing without the walls, in a clumsy old coach drawn at a foot's pace by six mules.

The Provincial Junta of Galicia was established here, and held their meetings in the town-hall, an ancient structure, the walls of which are covered with a profusion of curious arabesque ornaments. I had occasion to attend their sitting for the purpose of making some arrangements for the conveyance of military stores, and found their proceedings exceedingly dilatory. Indeed, on all occasions a lamentable degree of apathy seemed to pervade everything connected with the public service.

Baron During, the Lieutenant of my troop, was sent to reconnoitre the country betwixt Lugo and Vigo, attended by an old Spanish soldier, to act as guide and interpreter.

28th.—Halted at Lugo.

29th.—The division marched four leagues to Constantino, a miserable village at the foot of a range of mountains. The doorways of the hovels of this place were so low that we had great difficulty in getting our horses under cover.

30th.—To Las Nogales, four leagues. About

midway passed the *puente nueva*, a beautiful bridge of three arches, raised on stone pillars more than 100 feet above the bed of a rivulet. The road is here carried across a considerable ravine in a very picturesque situation. It is almost a continued ascent from Constantino, and there are many romantic spots betwixt Lugo and this place; but the prospect is in general tiresome from its uniformity, the hills being similar to each other in shape, and not broken into the abrupt outlines usual in mountainous countries. Instead of that variety we have here a regular succession of round hills, rising gradually behind each other, and separated by narrow valleys watered by small streams.

Nogales is a large village prettily situated at the base of a lofty mountain. The River Valcazar flows near the place, which is surrounded by well-cultivated fields and ornamented with fine trees. In summer it must be a delightful spot; but whilst we were there the weather was bad, the streets dirty, and the inhabitants so ill-disposed towards us that I was much annoyed at receiving directions to halt till further orders.

The determination to retreat, which had been suspended for a few days, was now acted upon,

and it is not surprising that our allies should have
formed unfavourable opinions of our intentions
from witnessing the indecision of our commanders.   To-day they might see troops and
stores hurried forward with the utmost despatch ;
to-morrow, perhaps, they would be marched back
again with equal precipitation.

December 1st.—Dined with Major Blackall, of
the 51st Regiment, and three or four infantry
officers who were stationed here in charge of
ammunition and stores.   In the evening I received orders to join the brigade as soon as
possible, with such men and horses only as were
fit for the most active service.   Whilst employed in
making the necessary arrangements for the march,
I was visited by two young Scotsmen who were
returning to their native country.   They told me
they had quitted the College of Valladolid, on
the general dispersion of the students a few days
before, in consequence of the approach of the
French army.   They assured me that the enemy
had met with no resistance, and that his advanced
guard, consisting of 8,000 men, entered the city
before they quitted it.

2nd.—Having selected the horses that appeared
fit for hard duty, which reduced the strength of

my detachment from 110 to 24, I proceeded to Trabadelos, a distance of seven leagues, where I found Cornet Phillips, who was on his way to Nogales to take the command of the division I had left there. In the course of this day's march we crossed a mountain above seven miles in ascent. Near the summit we met the 76th Regiment, which formed the advanced guard of our retreating army; the appearance of these troops, dimly seen through the mist as they wound round the hill, and the occasional gleams of sunshine reflected from their arms, had a very fine effect.

Trabadelos is a wretched village; here I first observed the charnel-house, which is common in the country churchyards. All the bones dug up in making fresh graves are deposited in these buildings, and seem to be carefully preserved. Several hundred skulls are often seen in one of these houses.

The 51st and 59th Regiments passed through the village soon after we had taken up our quarters.

3rd.—Marched two leagues to Villafranca, where we halted for a few hours to procure provisions and forage, and then continued our

8

route to Cacabelos, four leagues distant from Trabadelos.

Villafranca is beautifully situated in a hollow at the base of a high mountain, which appears to overhang the town. The approach from the north is beautiful and romantic; the road for some miles winds through a defile betwixt steep rocks, occasionally covered with wood; and the Burvia, a clear and rapid stream, runs in the bottom, sometimes rippling between smooth, green banks, and sometimes foaming over a rocky channel. This town belongs to the province of Leon, but stands on the borders of Galicia. There is an ancient castle here, which belonged to the ferocious Duke of Alva; it is a gloomy building, and I believe is generally used as a prison, but when I saw it, was occupied as a barrack by our men. The streets are narrow and dismal, and the buildings for the most part mean; there is, however, a monastery of Franciscans, which is a magnificent structure. The town was full of troops; it appeared to be a place of no trade.

I breakfasted with some officers of the 81st Regiment, and found that it was supposed to be the intention of Sir David Baird to throw up entrenchments on the heights, and maintain a position at Villafranca until Blake and Romana had recruited their armies, which had been almost annihilated in a series of disastrous actions in the province of Las Montanos. This plan appeared the most judicious that could be adopted, as the town is situated at the entrance of the strong mountain passes which continue almost without interruption to Constantino, a distance of twelve leagues; and the whole of this district presents obstacles to the advance of an army, which, in the presence of a resolute enemy, may be termed insurmountable.

Upon leaving Villafranca the prospect became more extensive, and we entered the level country called El Bierzo, in which Cacabelos is situated. This town stands on the left bank of the Cua, a river which, although nearly dry during the summer, in the rainy season, and when swollen by the melting of the snow in the mountains, is both broad and rapid, and often occasions considerable damage to the fields and vineyards. This tract of country is fertile, and there is more appearance of wealth and comfort amongst the inhabitants than can be found in any part of Galicia. The wine made in this district is chiefly white ; it is rather sweet, but has a pleasant flavour, and is infinitely superior in every respect to the *vino tinto* of the adjoining province.

The town bears strong marks of decay, and two sides of the plaza are in ruins. Sir David Baird and his staff passed through in the afternoon on their way to Villafranca.

4th.—The detachment assembled at daybreak and reached Bembibere, after a march of five leagues through a rich country beautifully varied with hill and dale, and in some places well wooded. I remarked several populous villages near the road ; the fields appeared well cultivated ; and a large proportion of the land was laid out in vineyards. We met several large droves of mules, laden chiefly with wine, which is carried in pigs' skins ; the seams are pitched, which often communicates a disagreeable flavour to the liquor. The muleteers are persons of great importance, and are treated with marked attention at the posadas. They wear a sort of cuirass of strong buff leather ; broad-brimmed hats ; and always travel well armed. Indeed, in this part of the country—which, by the way, is the scene of Gil Blas's adventures with the robbers—it is rare to meet any traveller, either mounted or on foot,

who does not carry a long firelock on the shoulder
or slung to the saddle.

Bembibere is a dirty, ugly town, one quarter
of which is completely in ruins. The River Sil
runs near it, and there is some very beautiful
scenery in the neighbourhood.

The 14th and 23rd Regiments, with a brigade
of artillery, were in quarters here, and some staff
officers, among whom I recognized several old
acquaintances. By clubbing our different messes
together we contrived to furnish a tolerably
good dinner—the first I had eaten since I left
Corunna. The wine was so bad that we could
not drink it, but a small stock of brandy and
rum which remained in my canteens enabled us
to spend the evening very jollily ; and when this
supply was exhausted, some regimental surgeons
who were of the party proposed spirits of wine
from the hospital stores as a substitute. The
experiment was tried, and the punch gave so
much satisfaction that the night was far advanced
before we separated.

A few French prisoners were brought into the
town in the afternoon and lodged in the gaol ; it
required a strong guard to protect them from
the fury of the populace, who were with difficulty

prevented from breaking into the prison and
butchering these unfortunate captives.

5th.—To Astorga, eight leagues. The road
for a considerable part of the distance passes
through a barren and dreary tract of country,
with scarcely any vestige of inhabitants or culti-
vation ; the mountains, however, afford pasturage
for numerous flocks of goats. The passes in this
range are almost as difficult as those near Villafranca, especially in the neighbourhood of Man-
zanal, four leagues from Bembibere, where, owing
to the extraordinary winding of the road, two
pieces of artillery, well served, would be sufficient
to check the progress of a numerous army. This
is the country of the Mauregatos, a distinct
tribe, differing in countenance, dress, and customs,
from the rest of the population. In some respects
they bear a resemblance to our gipsies, but are
happily free from the thieving propensities of
that vagabond race.

Astorga is situated in a sandy plain which
extends farther than the eye can reach ; there
are many populous villages in the vicinity. The
soil is very productive, and the bread made here
is remarkably white and good, whereas throughout the whole province of Galicia it is brown,

sour, and full of sand, which is attributed to the
softness of the millstones. This town is of great
antiquity; it stands on a small eminence, and
must have been a place of uncommon strength
in former ages. The ancient walls which still
remain are above 12 feet in thickness; the towers
are massive and lofty, and were probably erected
by the Moors when they were in possession of
the country. Caverns have been formed in the
foundations of the walls, which serve for the
habitations of a most miserable and squalid troop
of beggars, several of whom I observed lying in
the ditch quite naked, basking in the sunshine,
and employed in freeing each other from vermin.
The cathedral is a noble specimen of ancient
Gothic architecture; it is exceedingly rich in
jewels, plate, and other valuables, to the amount,
as I was assured, of half a million sterling; but
everything that could be removed had been
secreted, in order to be preserved from the
rapacity of the French, from whom the inhabitants expected a visit.

The convents and churches had been put in
requisition for the accommodation of the British
forces; our horses were stabled in the chapel of
a convent where the detachment was quartered,

and I found one of them tied to a large image of the Virgin, and some others fastened to a brazen font, which at the same time answered the purpose of a manger.   Considering the characteristic superstition and bigotry of the nation, I was astonished at the indifference with which the Spaniards witnessed the profanation of their sacred edifices by heretics.   The town contains several churches and convents; but it was late in the afternoon before we arrived, and I was then so much occupied in getting quarters for my party and making other necessary arrangements, that I had not leisure to take even a cursory view of them.   The place is gloomy, and the streets narrow and dirty, but the houses are large and tolerably well furnished.   The shops were well supplied with provisions and other necessaries, notwithstanding the consumption that must have been made by our army, which had been stationed in the neighbourhood for several days.   The cavalry and horse artillery had marched in the morning, leaving a great number of men with horses unfit for severe duty, who were to return to Corunna under the command of Colonel Quintin, of the 10th Hussars. In consequence of this and former deductions, the actual strength of each regiment could scarcely exceed 400 men mounted in the field.

I found a note from the Adjutant of the Fifteenth, with orders for me to join the regiment by ten o'clock the next morning, but without any directions where to find it, as the destination had been kept a profound secret, even from the General commanding the brigade. The discovery of their route was therefore left to my ingenuity.

The army of the Marquis de la Romana entered the town about four o'clock. The men were strangely equipped, and seemed quite undisciplined; they marched in file, moving in double-quick time, with a wretched drum at the head of each regiment. This force did not exceed 2,000 men, part of whom were dressed in English uniforms.

In the evening the greatest confusion and terror prevailed in the place on account of the approach of the enemy, who was reported to have entered Leon—ten leagues from Astorga—within twelve hours after Romana's corps quitted it. In consequence of this rumour the shops were shut up, and all the inhabitants who possessed the means of removal prepared for their departure by packing up their most valuable effects.

6th. — Being very anxious to overtake the brigade, I ordered my party to assemble before daylight, and, as the forward movement of the cavalry, under existing circumstances, could only be for the purpose of forming a junction with Sir John Moore's army, we took the road to Benevente, and at the end of four leagues reached La Baneza, a small town at the confluence of the Rivers Tuerta and Orbigo, where, to my great delight, I found the brigade. I have seldom experienced greater satisfaction than I felt on transferring the men of my detachment to their respective regiments. I had been heartily sick of my command from the very commencement of the march, for, although the conduct of the individuals of my own regiment was most exemplary, nothing could exceed the insubordination of the rest. They treated their non-commissioned officers with the most profound contempt, and I was on one occasion obliged to draw my sword on a private of the —— to enforce obedience to the order to turn out for a march.

The pleasure of rejoining my corps after a

separation which had appeared extremely tedious, was enhanced by the expectation of speedily coming into action, as it was supposed the French would occupy the towns of Benevente and Zamora, and secure the bridges across the Ezla and Duero before we could reach them; in which case it was Lord Paget's intention that we should cut our way through their line. It was the prevalent opinion that Sir John Moore would be forced to retire from Salamanca before we could arrive there, and that our march would, in consequence, be directed towards Portugal.

As the advanced parties of the enemy's cavalry were said to be in our neighbourhood, picquets were posted in all the avenues to the town, and the roads were patrolled in every direction; the hour and object of our march were also carefully concealed from the inhabitants. The bugles sounded " to horse " at eleven o'clock at night, when the troops assembled at the alarm post. There was a sharp frost, and we moved at a foot-pace, and halted frequently to wait for the reports of our reconnoitring parties, which occasioned us to feel the cold more sensibly.

7th.—The march to Benevente occupied nine hours, although the distance from La Baneza is

only six leagues. This is a walled town in an
extensive plain watered by the Ezla. I believe
the only thing particularly worthy of notice in
the place is a castle, which was formerly the
residence of the Counts of Benevente. It is a
magnificent specimen of Moorish and Gothic
architecture; the turrets are richly ornamented
with fretwork, and many of the towers have their
summits bound round with a massive chain
sculptured in the stone—a common ornament in
Moorish buildings. That front of the castle
which overlooks the plain is raised on ranges of
Moorish arches, supported by columns of por-
phyry and granite. I understood the interior
was fitted up in a style of equal magnificence,
but I had not leisure to examine it.

The streets are narrow, and the general appearance of the place is gloomy; but there was an
air of cleanliness and comfort in the houses which
I had not met with hitherto, and the shops were
well supplied with articles of provisions, etc.,
which were of the greatest necessity to men who
had been scantily fed and ill-lodged for several
days. The shopkeepers, however, took care to
make us pay an exorbitant price for what we
wanted. The population, which scarcely ex-

ceeds 4,000 souls, is by no means in proportion to the extent of the place.

The brigade was ordered to assemble at eleven o'clock, but it was considerably past midnight before we commenced our march, owing to the Seventh and Tenth mistaking the place of rendezvous.

8th.—At the distance of half a league from Benevente we crossed the Ezla by a noble stone bridge of several arches, and passed through Castro Gonzalo, a large village seated on the steep bank of the river. We had not proceeded far from this place when two or three blue lights were observed to rise at some distance, which were considered as signals made by the enemy's spies to give notice of our approach, as this was one of the points where we expected our progress to be interrupted. The regiments were in consequence directed to move in open column of divisions—or half-squadrons, whenever the ground would admit of it ; the greatest precautions were observed, and every individual was ordered to keep on the alert. We proceeded, however, unmolested, except by the severity of the cold, until nine o'clock, when we halted in a plain near the villages of Ruegos and Cabiera,

9

seven leagues from Benevente and five from
Zamora.

During this march I had an opportunity of
learning in what slight estimation our Brigadier
(General Slade) was held by the commander of
the cavalry.

Just after the blue lights had been noticed,
and whilst we were in momentary expectation
of an attack, Lord Paget rode along the flank of
the column giving directions respecting the order
of the march and precautions to be attended to,
which he desired the General to repeat to the
squadron officers of the Tenth; but no sooner
had Slade left him than his lordship called one
of his aides-de-camp, whom he ordered to "ride
after that damned stupid fellow" and take care
that he committed no blunder. This speech—
which, to say the least of it, was very ill-timed—
was made within hearing of a number of officers
and soldiers, and was calculated to deprive the
Brigadier even of the slight degree of respect
previously entertained for him by the troops.

As soon as we arrived on the ground we were
to occupy during the day, strong picquets were
detached in every direction; officers were despatched to reconnoitre, and foraging-parties sent

into the nearest villages. The horses were then unsaddled and picketed, and fires kindled for cooking and warming ourselves. In the forenoon a patrol of the Tenth reported that they had seen some French dragoons about three miles from our bivouac. They probably belonged to a foraging or an advanced post from the force at Rio Seco, and retired as soon as they noticed our patrol, for the picquet which was sent in search of them returned without success. The horses were saddled at sunset, and the column was formed at midnight.

9th.—This march was conducted with the same silence and precaution as the two former, and during the greater part of it neither officers nor men could keep their eyes open; the extreme cold, added to the fatigue of three night marches, caused a drowsiness which it was almost impossible to resist. The cold had been severe on the two former nights, but on this the frost was so intense that in the morning our fur caps were bristled with icicles. We entered Zamora* about seven o'clock, crossing the ditch by a temporary

* Turquoises were found in abundance in the neighbourhood, whence the town was named Medina Zamoratorio by the Moors.

bridge of planks, the stone bridge having been demolished to prevent the entrance of the enemy's cavalry, whose foragers had been scouring the adjacent country for some days past. Our reception here was of a nature to revive those ardent feelings in the cause of Spain which had been somewhat damped by the apathy we had witnessed since we left Corunna. The cannons on the ramparts roared for an hour after our arrival; drums beat and trumpets sounded in all quarters; and the streets were crowded with people shouting, "Vivan los Ingleses!" Every balcony was filled with ladies waving handkerchiefs, and even the nuns thrust their fair hands through the grated windows of their convents, and showered the warmest benedictions on their "brave defenders." In short, our progress through the streets resembled a triumphal procession.

The Junta gave a public breakfast to the officers, and the soldiers were feasted by the inhabitants upon whom they were quartered.

This city and Toro are the only places besides Corunna where there appeared a probability of the populace making a determined effort to resist the invaders; but any opposition they could have offered here must have been quickly overcome by regular troops, as there are no fortifications except an ancient stone wall and dry ditch, and the volunteers who composed the garrison were neither numerous nor well disciplined. The situation of the place also incapacitates it for defence, for, although it is protected on one side by the Duero, it is commanded by higher ground on the remaining quarters.

I was billeted with Captain Seelinger and Surgeon Lidderdale at the house of a hidalgo, who had filled some office in the household of Ferdinand before he succeeded to the crown. Our host treated us in the most hospitable manner, and sent an express to his country-seat for his wife and daughter, who had quitted the city to avoid the inconvenience of the expected attack from which our arrival secured it, that they might assist him in paying attention to the " English heroes," as he was pleased to term us. Every officer was treated with equal kindness, for the people seemed to vie with each other in hospitality to their allies. If the rest of the country had been animated with the same spirit that prevailed in the *corregimientos* of Zamora and Toro, I may venture to assert that the result of the campaign would have been far different ;

10

and very different, I am confident, would have
been the sentiments towards the Spaniards with
which we quitted the country.

Zamora is the see of a Bishop; it contains a
number of churches and convents, besides three
hospitals and other public buildings; but owing
to the short time we remained there, and the
portion that was necessarily devoted to military
duties and repose, I had no opportunity of ex-
amining any of them. The same causes frequently operated to prevent our seeing anything
worthy of notice in the places we passed through.

From the size of the town I should rate the
population at about 15,000 souls. There is a
handsome stone bridge across the Duero, which
is very broad at this spot, although 150 miles
from its mouth. Many of the streets are tolerably spacious, clean, and well paved; some of the
principal ones are lighted by lamps at night.
The town upon the whole seems rich and pros-
perous, and free from the appearances of desola-
tion and decay so generally to be seen in Spanish
towns. The houses are large and well furnished;
some of the apartments are provided with fire-
places, which is a very uncommon case in Spain,
where, except in the kitchen, the substitute for a

fire is usually a *brasero*—a brass pan filled with charcoal, around which the shivering natives sit, enveloped in the ample folds of their *capas* and inhaling the noxious vapours, but certainly gaining very little additional heat.

The surrounding country is in general flat, but occasionally swells into hills; the soil is sandy, and produces abundant crops. The wine made here is particularly good; it is a strong-bodied red wine, equal to port of the first quality.

10*th.*—We expected to halt here one day at least to refresh the horses; but at ten o'clock, just as we had sat down to a capital breakfast, we were surprised by the unwelcome sound of " Boots and saddles," and within an hour bade adieu to Zamora, which we left with regret, and proceeded to Toro, six leagues distant. On the march we passed through Fresno, a large village, and traversed an extensive wood of cork-trees and dwarf evergreen oaks. The road is generally carried near the banks of the river, which in many places are steep and picturesque. On approaching Toro the country becomes more hilly, and is chiefly laid out in vineyards; the town is seated on the summit of a very steep ascent on the right bank of the Duero, over which it has a noble stone bridge of many arches. On the banks of a small river which falls into the Duero at a short distance below the bridge, there are several fulling-mills, which have a very pretty effect, as the buildings are whitewashed and stand amidst gardens and vineyards.

Toro is a large town, not inferior in size to Zamora, and contains a number of churches and religious edifices, many of which are of great antiquity. The place is surrounded by a mud wall and defended by an ancient castle; but little dependence can be placed on these fortifications. It is, however, much more capable of defence than Zamora from its situation, and the citizens were actuated by the same spirit of loyalty to Ferdinand and hatred to the French; the latter feeling was even more lively amongst *them*, as they had been subjected a short time before to the insolence and oppression of a French garrison.

During this day's march I commanded the advance guard, which was met above a mile from the town by a great concourse of people, chiefly of the lower classes, who saluted us with " vivas." It was late in the evening before we entered the place, and as we passed through the streets many of the inhabitants displayed lights in their windows; but when we reached the plaza we found it completely illuminated. Flambeaux were ranged on every balcony; an immense crowd was assembled in the square and adjoining streets; and the windows were filled with ladies waving their handkerchiefs, and crying, " Vivan los Ingleses," which we returned by exclamations of " Viva Fernando VIImo !" " Viva Spana !"

The quartermasters had not been sent forward in time to provide billets for the troops, but every house was open to the soldiers, and the owners exerted themselves to make us comfortable. I lodged at the house of a physician, who treated me with great hospitality. He complained bitterly of the conduct of two French officers, who had been billeted at his house during the summer. In the course of the evening the conversation turned on the subject of religion, and I was obliged to explain to my host the points wherein the Protestant faith differs from the Roman Catholic; but I fear my illustrations only led him into error, as he arrived at the conclusion that there is no material difference between the tenets of the two Churches. This mistake, however, had the effect of increasing the cordiality of the whole family towards me.

As I had been obliged to leave my breakfast half finished, and had tasted nothing since, I was rather impatient for the arrival of the supper hour, and saw the table covered with much satisfaction. The dishes consisted chiefly of pork, dressed in different ways, but always with abundance of oil and garlic; hog's puddings; and an *olla podrida*.

The next morning, when I came downstairs, I found the lady of the house taking her chocolate in bed in the common sitting-room. Feeling rather abashed at what I considered an intrusion into her apartment, I was about to retire, but was desired by her husband to remain and pay my respects to the lady. I mentioned this circumstance to Major Leitch, who told me that at his quarters there was a *tertulla*, and, upon his expressing his wish to go to rest, he was shown a bed within a recess in the same room where the company was assembled, and desired to undress without ceremony. A Spaniard's breakfast is a very poor apology for that meal, being nothing more than a small cup of chocolate and a thin slice of toasted bread or a sugared biscuit. It is frequently taken in bed, and they seem to consider this early breakfast of great consequence to the preservation of their health, and never go abroad in the morning fasting if they can avoid it.

Toro is a very gloomy place; the streets are in general narrow and excessively dirty; the mud was above a foot deep, although there had been no rain for several days, and the stench that proceeded from this congregation of every sort of filth was most abominable; it was, besides, impossible to cross a street without wading through this mass of corruption.

The swine here are of immense size and exceeding fat; they are allowed to go at large through the town and wallow in the mud all day long, which perhaps causes the superiority of the Toro pork. I never met with well-fed mutton or beef, but the pork was invariably good. The shops here were tolerably well stocked, but the tradespeople were by no means moderate in their demands upon our purses, notwithstanding their patriotism. Leathern bottles and skins for keeping wine (*borachos*) seemed to be the chief articles of manufacture.

11*th*.—About two o'clock in the afternoon the

left squadron of the Fifteenth marched to occupy Morales, a small town one league from Toro, on the road to Valladolid. Information had been received that bodies of French cavalry were stationed at Rio Seco and Rueda, in consequence of which we were kept on the alert; and at midnight I was roused from my bed and sent to post a picquet at Villa Vendemia, about a league from Morales, in the direction of Villalpando. Three Spaniards on foot accompanied us as guides; but on attempting to find the way back, after executing the duty I had been sent upon, I missed the road, which was merely a track in the sand, and wandered about on the plain above two hours before I got to my quarters.

12th.—At three o'clock in the afternoon I was detached with my own troop to occupy the village of Villa Vendemia, in order to patrol the roads in the direction of Rio Seco, and communicate during the night with the picquets from Toro, Morales, and Pedrosa del Rey. I took up my abode at the house of the Alcalde, with whom I drank a cup of wine the night before when I came to post the picquet. Señor Bartoleo, my host, was a substantial farmer, whose person resembled the description given of the renowned squire of " Don Quixote." He seemed good-tempered and hospitable ; his wife was an agreeable woman, but without any pretensions to beauty. Indeed, notwithstanding the reputation of this country for female beauty, the number of handsome women I have seen is very limited. They have in general fine, expressive dark eyes, and often neat feet and ankles, without anything else in their personal appearance to attract admiration.

Bartoleo's house, like the generality of the habitations belonging to the peasants in the plains, had low mud walls and a thatched roof ; but the interior was sufficiently commodious, clean, and comfortably furnished. The bed I slept in was remarkably good, but so short that I could not stretch myself in it. One might be tempted to imagine that the Spaniards are measured for beds as well as for clothes, and, as they are usually of diminutive stature, we always found their beds deficient in length. The superior height and fine appearance of the British soldiers struck them with admiration, and both men and women, as we passed through their towns and villages, continually exclaimed : " What tall, stout, handsome men !"

The sight of Bartoleo's kitchen made me almost fancy myself in an English farmhouse. There was a blazing fire on the hearth, which was piled with logs of wood instead of being made with chaff or cow-dung kneaded into cakes with clay, which is often the only fuel to be procured. The walls were whitewashed, and garnished with numerous cooking utensils perfectly bright and clean. From the ceiling hung the carcasses of above fifty sheep, goats, and hogs—chined and dried or salted—with a plentiful stock of black puddings and sausages; and a large quantity of bread, baked for winter provision, of rye and Indian corn.

The parish priest and a student from Salamanca supped with us; the former was so much smitten with the hussar uniform that he put on my pelisse and fur cap, in which he strutted about the kitchen, and, drawing my sabre, he flourished it over his head, to the great dismay of the women and imminent danger of the links of black puddings and sausages. We had an excellent supper, highly seasoned with garlic, but I was by this time too much accustomed to Spanish cookery to be fastidious; besides, our opportunities of getting a good meal were so precarious that it would have been highly imprudent to let one slip. The farmer's wife waited upon us, and did not sit down to her own supper until we had finished.

I cannot tell whether it was owing to their keeping but few cattle in the plains of Castille and Leon, or that they were housed for the winter, but we seldom saw any in the fields, and I never could procure cow's milk after we left Galicia. A substance they called " butter " was lard preserved in pig's gut, and too rancid to be eatable ; it is used by the natives in cookery as a substitute for oil. I may here observe that we found the oil in general very bad, owing to the slovenly manner in which it is manufactured, as the Spaniards do not even take the trouble to pick out the rotten or unripe olives.

13*th*.—I was relieved in the afternoon by a squadron of the Seventh, and received orders to return to Morales, where I found the regiment assembled, with the exception of the right squadron, which was detached to Villa Don Alonzo, a league and a half in advance.

A considerable quantity of wine of an excellent quality is made in this district. The wine-cellars — *bodegas* — are sunk to a considerable depth underground, and so constructed as to be warm in winter and cool in summer. They are usually excavated in convenient situations near the towns and villages, and from a little distance have the appearance of a range of low hills. Notwithstanding the fastenings to the doors are very slight, I believe instances of their being robbed were of rare occurrence until a British army traversed the country.

At Morales I was billeted in the house of Manuel de la Peña, a farmer, where I found a few books, and amongst them the translation of an English novel, called " Louisa ; or, The Cottage on the Moor." Although I can only describe Señors Bartoleo and Manuel as farmers, I dare say they are both hidalgos with pedigrees from the time of Pelagius at least. In the evening I was favoured with the company of half a dozen friars ; their ignorance on every subject of conversation was such that I could not even obtain from them the most trifling information respecting the country in the immediate vicinity. I showed them my pocket map of Spain, which excited so much admiration that I am convinced they had never seen one before. It cost me at least a quarter of an hour's labour to make them comprehend the relative position of some of the principal Spanish towns. But it was quite beyond my power to make them understand the situation of the British Isles, which they were very anxious to ascertain; or to persuade them that our country is separated both from France and Spain by the ocean.

These friars, and, indeed, the people in general, were very inquisitive respecting the cost of our dress and appointments, and desirous to learn whether the buttons and lace of our pelisses were silver. I was also repeatedly questioned as to my rank in the service and the pay attached to it; on these occasions I always caused great astonishment by stating the pay of a captain of cavalry at 30,000 reals per annum.

Before supper two of the farmer's servants performed the fandango, to my great amusement. They danced to the music of a *tambour de Basque*, accompanied by the voice, and snapped their fingers to imitate the sound of the castanets. They wore wooden shoes, and moved round the room in slow time with the most perfect gravity, whilst their ludicrous attempts to display the graces of the dance were diverting beyond measure.

11

CHAPTER III

[*On December* 9 *Colonel Graham, who had been
sent by Moore to Madrid to find out what was really
taking place in the capital, returned with the news
that a capitulation had already been signed, and
Moore thereupon determined to effect his junction
with Baird at Valladolid, thereafter acting as circumstances might dictate. Three days later Moore
communicated to Baird his intention, already noted
in his diary of the* 11th, *of moving upon Palencia
and Burgos, in order to make a diversion in favour
of the Spaniards by threatening the French communications; at this period the Commander of the British
Forces was under the impression that the French
armies in Spain comprised no more than, at most,*
90,000 *men, that the people of Madrid were hot for
resistance, and that the Spanish armies still mustered*
60,000 *strong.*

On December 13 *Moore was at Alaejos, where he
was handed the famous intercepted despatch from
Berthier to Soult, which opened Moore's eyes—not*

*only to the risks of prosecuting his projected move-
ment on Burgos, but to the immense numerical
superiority of the French forces in Spain; at the
same time it showed him plainly that Soult on the
Carrion was weak and isolated, and was open to
attack and rout before he could be supported from the
south or east. On the 15th Moore crossed the Douro
and moved upon Mayorga, being joined by Baird at
Valderas, where the whole combined army was re-
distributed.*

*Soult had in the meantime become aware of the
movements of the British, and had called his two
infantry divisions together at Saldana and Carrion,
covered by his cavalry at Sahagun and Riberos ; on
the night of December 20-21 Lord Paget surprised
and overwhelmed Debelle's cavalry brigade at the
former place.]*

December 14*th.*—The Light Brigade of Sir
John Moore's army passed through Morales at
one o'clock, and we received orders soon afterwards to march to Tordesillas, five leagues
distant. We did not arrive there until eight
o'clock, and the roads were so slippery, owing
to the severity of the frost, that we could scarcely
keep our horses on their legs. It was quite dark
when we entered the town, and large bonfires

were burning in the streets; lights were also displayed at the windows and doors of many of the houses. The populace greeted us with "vivas," but we were not received with the same enthusiasm as was shown at Zamora and Toro. It was even asserted that the bonfires were made by persons in the French interest to enable spies, who were placed in different parts of the town, to take an accurate account of our force for the enemy's information.

A short time before our arrival twenty-four French hussars were in the town for several hours, and obtained a considerable quantity of forage and provisions, all their requisitions being complied with in a place containing at least 4,000 inhabitants, although the army of their allies was only a few leagues distant. Information of the circumstance was, indeed, sent to our advanced squadron at Villa Don Alonzo; but the enemy were allowed to retire with their booty before the picquet which was despatched to intercept them had time to arrive. This was not a very favourable specimen of the courage of a people who, we had flattered ourselves, were capable of contending with the veteran troops of France; but repeated instances of the same kind occurred to prove that, however strong their professions of hatred to the invaders, the presence of a mere handful of French troops was at any time sufficient to convert the hostility of the most populous towns into submission. Indeed, I never saw anything in the conduct of the Spaniards that denoted valour; on the contrary, from the few opportunities I have had of forming an opinion on the subject, I should conclude them to be a remarkably timid nation.

Tordesillas is situated on the right bank of the Duero, over which it has a fine stone bridge of ten arches; the centre is occupied by a large tower. One half of the plaza is in ruins, and every quarter of the town presents the strongest signs of poverty and decay. The place is not fortified, but would make a strong position, as it commands the river and adjacent country. The only public buildings I saw, besides the churches, were a large hospital and a very fine convent dedicated to St. Clare, which stands near the bridge. The wine made in this neighbourhood is excellent, and very much resembles champagne; it would be much improved if it were bottled instead of being kept in *borachos* and casks.

12

The whole of the cavalry was assembled here; the 18th Hussars and 3rd Hussars of the German Legion, who had marched from Portugal with Sir John Hope's column, arrived soon after us; a party of the former regiment having on the preceding day surprised a detachment of the enemy's cavalry at Rueda, a small town two leagues from hence on the opposite side of the Duero, when several waggons laden with cotton, said to be worth £80,000, fell into the hands of the victors. The greater part of the French—who were superior in number to their opponents—were killed or made prisoners. The loss of the Eighteenth was inconsiderable, and several of them appeared on parade next day equipped with the broad buff belts and gauntlet gloves of the French dragoons, which caused some repining amongst our men at the superior luck of the Eighteenth. Orders were given out this evening for the cavalry to proceed to Simancas, a town on the borders of Old Castille, six leagues from Tordesillas; but in the morning there was a change of plan at headquarters—in consequence of the information contained in an intercepted letter from Berthier to Soult*—and after being kept in suspense for

* For the terms of this letter see Appendix I.

some hours our destination was fixed for La
Motta.

15th.—The brigade divided on the march.
General Slade halted with the Fifteenth at La
Motta, four leagues from Tordesillas; the other
regiments occupied St. Cyprien, Valmoase,
Pedrosa del Rey, and Villa Don Diego.   On the
route we passed through the town of Vega, near
which place some horsemen were observed on
an eminence.   As they had a suspicious appearance, a party was despatched to discover what
they were, but was unable to overtake them.

La Motta is a small town situated in the
midst of sandhills, which abound in this part of
the country; the plain is much intersected by
deep and wide ditches, and scarcely a single tree
is to be seen for a distance of many leagues.
This town was formerly walled round and
defended by a strong castle, the foundations
of which may be traced and enclose a considerable space.   One of the towers is still standing,
the walls of which are very massive and in good
repair.

We found on our arrival that the Junta had
issued a proclamation forbidding the inhabitants
to take any money from the English, and I had

great difficulty in prevailing on a poor woman, from whom I bought some chestnuts, to receive the payment I offered.

The weather continued to be very fine for the season, and the temperature of the air during the day was sufficiently warm ; but the nights were intensely cold, and the severity of the frost often made the roads dangerous.

We mounted a picquet of a hundred men, as the enemy's cavalry was stated to be in force at Valladolid and Palencia, which made it necessary for us to be on our guard. Lieutenant Carpenter, who was one of the subalterns on duty, having been sent to visit the vedettes and patrols about midnight, I was informed soon afterwards that his horse had returned without a rider, upon which I despatched some hussars in search of the Lieutenant. He soon made his appearance at our fire, and related his adventures, which afforded us a hearty laugh at his expense. It appeared that, in withdrawing his leg from under his horse, which had slipped up with him, he left his boot behind ; and after looking for it a long time in vain, when he attempted to remount, the Camel, which was the name his charger had obtained, broke loose and galloped off, leaving his master to hop back without a boot. He complained that his foot was almost frozen, and grievously lamented his loss, but in the morning the boot was discovered fixed in the stirrup!

The night passed without any alarm, and I took out a small party before daybreak in the hope of surprising a French picquet, which, from the reports of our patrols, I had reason to believe was stationed a few miles off, on the road to Rio Seco, but was obliged to give up the search, after riding about for two hours, without discovering any traces of an enemy having been in the neighbourhood. A party which had been sent in the direction of Valladolid on a similar errand was equally unsuccessful.

16th.—The regiment halted at La Motta on the 16th.

The only building I saw there worth notice is a palace belonging to the Duke of Alva, who has very extensive possessions in this part of the country. The Duke, who is a minor, does not reside there, but the house is inhabited by an *intendante*, whose wife and sisters were the most beautiful women I had yet seen in Spain. Some of the officers who went to view the building were invited to dinner, when a sumptuous repast was provided, after which we danced minuets, country-dances, and waltzes, but could not prevail upon the ladies to favour us with an exhibition of the fandango. The music was very indifferent, the only instruments being a miserable spinet and a square tambourine covered with parchment on both sides, and without bells. The palace is a large stone edifice in a plain style of architecture; the walls of a gallery which overlooks the gardens are covered with a series of ludicrous paintings, not of the most delicate description, in which nuns and monks are the principal characters.

17*th*.—We marched this day to Villa Graxima, which by the direct road is only three leagues from La Motta; but General Slade, with his wonted sagacity, contrived to find out a route which increased the distance by two leagues. We passed through Valmoase, where we were received with " vivas," and noticed several small towns and villages to our right and left, but I do not recollect their names; they were all situated on elevated ground, and one of them— St. Cyprien, I believe — was defended by a Moorish castle, the walls and towers of which appeared in complete repair.

Villa Graxima is a small town containing nothing worth notice except a handsome church; the inhabitants received us hospitably, and seemed anxious to make us as comfortable as their slender means would allow.

Maria Antonia de Barbadillo y Castro, the daughter of a hidalgo at whose house I was quartered, was a very beautiful and agreeable young woman. Almost every moment of my brief sojourn at Villa Graxima was devoted to this lady, and I employed my stock of Spanish compliments and flattering speeches with such success that, at parting, she made me promise to write to her, and engaged to accompany me to England when we returned from driving the Gallic invaders out of Spain! The unfortunate issue of the campaign rendered these engagements nugatory, and I cannot reflect without pain on the probable fate of this interesting girl, subjected as the province has since been to the brutal excesses of the French soldiery.

About 600 of the enemy's cavalry were stationed at Medina del Rio Seco, one league from this place, and a party of their foragers—by whose exertions we profited—were employed here when our quartermasters, who preceded the regiment to provide billets, appeared in sight, upon which they retired with precipitation to give the alarm. After our picquets were posted, Colonel Grant and some of the officers rode to Rio Seco, and were met by a great concourse of the inhabitants, who informed them, with great exultation, that the French had decamped an hour before, taking the road to Palencia. They effected their retreat in a most admirable manner, without leaving a single man, horse, or article of baggage behind, notwithstanding the shortness of the notice.

We had great reason on this occasion to lament the want of enterprise displayed by our worthy Brigadier, and his total neglect of all means to procure information ; it was an unfortunate circumstance that he had chosen to attach himself to the Fifteenth, for if he had remained with the Tenth I have little doubt that Colonel Grant would have given us an opportunity of proving our mettle.

The country is quite level about Villa Graxima, but swells into hills in the immediate neighbourhood of Rio Seco. I was told by a Spaniard, who boasted of having been present and wounded in the action, that his countrymen occupied the heights previous to the battle fought there last July.* He added that in the early part of the day the advantage was on their side; flushed with this partial success, they imprudently quitted their position, and descended into the plain, which exposed them to the charge of the French cavalry. They were in consequence defeated with immense slaughter, but not until they had occasioned a loss of 6,000 men to the conquerors. I merely state this account without pretending to vouch for its accuracy.

18*th.*—This being Sunday, we expected to have remained quiet at Villa Graxima, and I accompanied my fair friend to matins; but whilst we were in the church the bugles sounded " Boots and saddles !" orders having arrived for the regiment to march to Villalpando, six leagues distant, and in less than three hours we were drawn up at the alarm-post outside the town. Here I took leave of my señorita, who, attended by a duenna, came to see the parade. As this march to Villalpando was decidedly a retrograde movement, it caused considerable discontent, although we endeavoured to persuade ourselves

* On the 14th of that month Cuesta was defeated by Bessières.—Ed.

it was only directed with the view of concentrating our forces. At two leagues from Villa Graxima we passed Torre de Humos, a small town on the banks of the Rio Seco, where there are the remains of a noble Moorish castle ; the place belongs to the Duke of Alva.

It was nearly dark when we arrived at Villalpando, and, as the town was quite filled with British troops, it was late in the evening before the regiment was provided with quarters ; and, after all, our accommodations were so bad that we might as well have remained in the streets. The horses were crowded into the cloisters of a convent, where they had scarcely room to stand, and the hussars could neither get straw to lie upon nor fire to cook their rations. Major Leitch and myself were billeted at a miserable hovel, where about twenty of the Rifle Corps were quartered ; and there were so many different messes cooking at the same time that it was ten o'clock before we could get any dinner.

Here we first heard the news of the surrender of Madrid, and I conversed with some Spanish soldiers who had been engaged in the conflict which preceded the capitulation. They attributed all their disasters to the incapacity and treason of their commanders, and boasted of their own individual achievements.

It was the general opinion that, in consequence of the unfortunate situation of affairs in Castille, our army would immediately fall back upon Portugal, but we were most agreeably surprised by receiving orders to advance in the direction of Burgos. Villalpando is a dirty, miserable-looking place; many of the houses are built of mud, and the inhabitants displayed, both in their persons and dwellings, a degree of dirt and poverty to which we had been strangers for some time.

19th.—Ever since the beginning of the month the weather had been colder than it usually is in England at this season, but for the last five or six days the frost had become most intense and the roads very slippery. The cavalry, horse artillery, and some brigades of infantry, assembled at eight o'clock, and marched in company to Valderas, a distance of five leagues, where the infantry and General Stewart's brigade of hussars halted. Our route lay through an open country, generally level, but occasionally rising into hills; the whole district presented a most dreary prospect, without a tree or even a shrub to enliven it, but the snow-capped mountains of Leon, which bounded the view, formed a grand horizon.

Our brigade, with the horse artillery, after separating from the rest of the division at Valderas, marched three leagues farther, and it was quite dark before we arrived at Mayorga. Having been eleven hours on the march, we remained on horseback in the streets above an hour, exposed to a heavy fall of snow, whilst the quartermasters were arranging the billets. It continued snowing all night, and in the morning the ground was covered to the depth of 8 or 10 inches.

20*th*.—We marched from Mayorga at ten o'clock. The Tenth and horse artillery halted at Melgar de Arriba, two leagues from our last quarters, where there is a fine convent, in which we had the good fortune to deposit General Slade, who seemed happy to take shelter from a heavy fall of snow in a place which promised such comfortable accommodations. The Fifteenth proceeded a league farther to Melgar de Abaxo, a dirty, miserable village, the inhabitants of which did not appear to rejoice much in our company. Many of them deserted their dwellings on our approach, taking especial care, however, to leave their doors and windows well secured ; in consequence of which we were obliged to break open several of the houses, a mode of proceeding that increased at the same time both the ill-will and the civility of the people who remained in the place. They no longer dared to show any marks of dislike to their visitors, but contented themselves with bewailing their misfortunes and imploring the succour of their favourite saints, devoutly crossing themselves whilst they freely consigned the bodies and souls of the *maldetos hereticos* to the guardianship of his Satanic Majesty. The Junta here appeared to be no better affected towards us than the rest of the population.

The officers commanding troops and squadrons were summoned to Colonel Grant's quarters at ten o'clock in the evening, when he acquainted us that Lord Paget had directed the regiment to be formed in readiness to march on a particular service precisely at midnight, and that we should probably be engaged with the enemy before daylight.

The Colonel ordered the troops to be assembled as silently as possible at eleven o'clock, and cautioned us to keep the Spaniards in ignorance

13

of the intended march, that they might not have it in their power to give information to the enemy. The regiment was formed at the hour appointed, but owing to the irregular manner in which we had been obliged to take up our quarters, and the bugles not being allowed to sound, several men were left behind whom the non-commissioned officers had not informed of the order to turn out. Lieutenant Buckley, who had joined us in the evening with a number of men and horses that had been left in Galicia, remained in the village to follow with the baggage and ineffectives in the morning.

21*st*.—Whilst we were drawn up at the alarm-post, waiting for the arrival of Lord Paget, a fire broke out in the village, occasioned, probably, by the carelessness of some of our dragoons. The glare of the flames partially illuminated the ground where we stood, and contrasted finely with the dark mass of our column ; whilst the melancholy sound of the church bell, which was struck*

* In all the churches and convents I had opportunities of seeing, the bells, which are without clappers, do not swing, but are fixed. The sexton goes up to the belfry to sound them by striking quick strokes with an iron rod, which produces a sound more like the clattering of fire-irons, or pots and pans, than the music of the bells.

to rouse the sleeping inhabitants, broke the silence of the night, and, combined with the object and probable consequences of our expedition, made the whole scene peculiarly awful and interesting.

Captain Thornhill, of the Seventh, who attended Lord Paget, with ten or twelve orderlies of his regiment, rode beside me during part of the night, and told me the object of our movement was to surprise a body of cavalry and artillery posted in a convent at Sahagun, a large town on the Cea, five leagues from Melgar de Abaxo. I afterwards learned that General Slade was directed to attack the convent with the Tenth and Horse Artillery, whilst the Fifteenth was to make a circuit and form on the opposite side of the town, in order to intercept their retreat. This plan, however, was rendered abortive by the bad state of the roads and the dilatory proceedings of the Brigadier, who on this occasion is reported to have made a long speech to the troops, which he concluded with the energetic peroration of " Blood and slaughter—march !"

Our march was disagreeable, and even dangerous, owing to the slippery state of the roads ; there was seldom an interval of many minutes without two or three horses falling, but fortunately few of their riders were hurt by these falls. The snow was drifted in many places to a considerable depth, and the frost was extremely keen. We left Melgar in the midst of a heavy fall of snow, and when that ceased I observed several vivid flashes of lightning.

We passed through two small towns or villages ; in one of these, about two leagues from Sahagun, is a noble castle, which appeared to great advantage " by the pale moonlight." Near this place our advanced guard came upon the enemy's picquet, which they immediately charged ; the Frenchmen ran away, and in the pursuit both parties fell into a deep ditch filled with snow. Two of the enemy were killed, and six or eight made prisoners; the remainder escaped and gave the alarm to the troops at Sahagun. Just at this period, when despatch was particularly required, our progress was very much impeded by two long narrow bridges,* without parapets, and

* In the atlas of the roads through Spain which accompanies De la Borde's statistical account of the country, Calzada de Sahagun and Calzada de los Hermanillos are marked at the distance of about a league from Sahagun. It was probably these causeways which impeded our advance so much on the morning of December 21, by obliging the

covered with ice, which we were obliged to cross in single file.

On our arrival at Sahagun we made a detour, to avoid passing through the streets, and discovered the enemy formed in a close column of squadrons near the road to Carrion de los Condes ; but, owing to the darkness of the morning and a thin mist, we could neither distinguish the number nor the description of the force opposed to us, further than to ascertain it consisted of cavalry.

Lord Paget immediately ordered us to form open column of divisions and trot, as the French, upon our coming in sight, made a flank movement, apparently with the intention of getting away ; but the rapidity of our advance soon convinced them of the futility of such an attempt. They therefore halted, deployed from column of squadrons, and formed a close column of regiments, which, as it is their custom to tell off in three ranks, made their formation six deep. During the time the two corps were moving in a parallel direction, the enemy's flankers, who

---

regiment to break into single file, and which, owing to the darkness, appeared to me like narrow bridges without parapets.

came within twenty or thirty yards of our column, repeatedly challenged, " Qui vive ?" but did not fire, although they received no answer. As soon as the enemy's order of battle was formed, they cheered in a very gallant manner, and immediately began firing. The Fifteenth then halted, wheeled into line, huzzaed, and advanced. The interval betwixt us was perhaps 400 yards, but it was so quickly passed that they had only time to fire a few shots before we came upon them, shouting : " Emsdorff and victory !" The shock was terrible ; horses and men were overthrown, and a shriek of terror, intermixed with oaths, groans, and prayers for mercy, issued from the whole extent of their front.

Our men, although surprised at the depth of the ranks, pressed forward until they had cut their way quite through the column. In many places the bodies of the fallen formed a complete mound of men and horses, but very few of our people were hurt. Colonel Grant, who led the right centre squadron, and the Adjutant who attended him, were amongst the foremost who penetrated the enemy's mass ; they were both wounded—the former slightly on the forehead, the latter severely in the face. It is probable

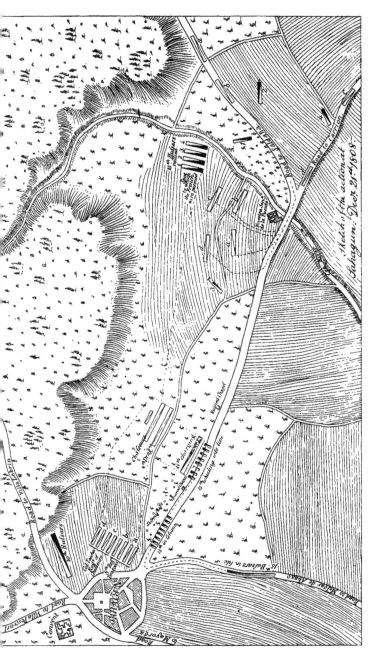

PLAN OF THE ACTION AT SAHAGUN.

To face page 102.

neither of them would have been hurt if our fur caps had been hooped with iron like those of the French Chasseurs, instead of being stiffened with pasteboard.

It was allowed, by everyone who witnessed the advance of the Fifteenth, that more correct movements, both in column and in line, were never performed at a review; every interval was accurately kept, and the dressing admirably preserved, notwithstanding the disadvantages under which we laboured. The attack was made just before daybreak, when our hands were so benumbed with the intense cold that we could scarcely feel the reins or hold our swords. The ground was laid out in vineyards intersected by deep ditches and covered with snow. Our horses, which had suffered from confinement on shipboard, change of forage, and the fatigues of incessant marches in inclement weather, were not in their usual condition; and, as the commanding officer had neglected to halt the regiment during the march for the purpose of tightening their girths, they had become so slack that when we began to gallop several of the blankets slipped from under the saddles.

The French were well posted, having a ditch

in their front, which they expected to check the impetus of our charge; in this, however, they were deceived. Lord Paget misjudged the distance or halted the Fifteenth too soon, by which means our right was considerably outflanked, and we outflanked theirs by a squadron's length. It was said afterwards that he intended the left squadron should have remained in reserve to support the charge, but no explicit order to that effect reached us. After the horses had begun to gallop, indeed, the word of command, " Left squadron to support !" was passed from the centre, but so indistinctly that Major Leitch did not feel authorized to act upon it, and at that moment we were so near the enemy that it would have been difficult to restrain either the men or horses.

My post being on the left of the line, I found nothing opposed to my troop, and therefore ordered, " Left shoulders forward !" with the intention of taking the French column in flank; but when we reached the ground they had occupied, we found them broken and flying in all directions, and so intermixed with our hussars that, in the uncertain twilight of a misty morning, it was difficult to distinguish friend from foe.

Notwithstanding this there was a smart firing of pistols, and our lads were making good use of their sabres. Upon reaching the spot where the French column had stood, I observed an officer withdrawn from the mêlée. I followed, and, having overtaken him, was in the act of making a cut at him which must have cleft the skull, when I thought I distinguished the features of Lieutenant Hancox; and, as I then remarked that he wore a black fur cap and a cloak which, in the dim light of the morning, looked like blue, I was confirmed in the idea that he belonged to our regiment. Under this impression, although his conduct in quitting the field at such a period struck me as very extraordinary, I sloped my sword, and merely exclaiming: "What, Hancox! is it you? I took you for a Frenchman!" turned my horse and galloped back to the scene of action. The shock I felt from the idea that I had been on the point of destroying a brother officer instead of an enemy deprived me of all inclination to use my sword except in defence of my own life; and the hostility I had cherished against the French only a few minutes before was converted into pity for them. When I met with Hancox after the action, I found that he wore an oilskin cover on his cap, and was not the person I had followed, who, I conclude, was an officer of the *grenadiers à cheval* or *compagnie d'élite*, which is attached to each regiment of dragoons in the French service, and doubtless was much astonished at my sudden appearance and abrupt departure. For my own part, I shall always consider it a most fortunate circumstance that I was thus deceived, since I have escaped the feeling of remorse to which I should have been exposed had I taken that man's life.

Many mistakes of the same kind must have occurred in the confusion after the charge. One of our men told me that I had a narrow escape myself, for that during the mêlée he had his sword raised to cut me down, but luckily recognized his officer in time to withhold the stroke.

At this time I witnessed an occurrence which afforded a good deal of amusement to those who were near the place. Hearing the report of a pistol close behind me, I looked round and saw one of the Fifteenth fall. I concluded the man was killed, but was quickly undeceived by a burst of laughter from his comrades, who exclaimed that the awkward fellow had shot his own horse, and many good jokes passed at his expense.

The mêlée lasted about ten minutes, the enemy always endeavouring to gain the Carrion road. The appearance of their heavy dragoons was extremely martial and imposing ; they wore brass helmets of the ancient Roman form, and the long black horsehair streaming from their crests as they galloped had a very fine effect.

Having rode together nearly a mile, pell-mell, cutting and slashing each other, it appeared to me indispensable that order should be re-established, as the men were quite wild and the horses almost blown ; therefore, seeing no superior officer near, I pressed through the throng until I overtook and halted those who were farthest advanced in pursuit. As soon as I had accomplished this object, the bugles sounded the " rally." Whilst we were re-forming our squadrons, the enemy also rallied and continued their flight by different routes. Our left and left centre squadrons were detached in pursuit of the *chasseurs à cheval*, who took the road to Carrion ; the other two squadrons followed the dragoons, who retired in the direction of Saldana.

Lord Paget accompanied the left centre squadron, and allowed the body he pursued to escape by sending an officer, with a white handkerchief as a flag of truce, to propose to them to surrender. The French took advantage of the delay this occasioned, and gained so great a start as to render further pursuit hopeless. The left squadron was more successful, and made about seventy prisoners, amongst whom were a Lieutenant-Colonel and three other officers ; but we could not prevent the escape of the main body, which, although more than double our number, never attempted to face us. Soon after our left squadron was put in motion in pursuit of the *chasseurs à cheval*, Baron Tripp came up to us and said that Lord Paget had sent him to desire the commanding officer to ride forward with a flag of truce and propose to them to surrender. Major Leitch made no answer, but, as if he had misunderstood the order, immediately gave the word of command to " Gallop !" upon which the squadron rushed on, leaving the Aide-de-Camp petrified with astonishment. It was entirely owing to Major Leitch's judicious conduct, in declining to act upon the flag of truce system, that his squadron was enabled to secure so many prisoners.

Whilst we were engaged in the pursuit of this division, my mare fell with me in leaping a very wide ditch, and floundered in a snow-wreath on the farther side ; my foot hung in the stirrup, and, being encumbered with my cloak, it was some time before I could extricate myself. The mare in the meantime ran away, leaving me in no very enviable situation.

Whilst I was following the squadron on foot, after having been dismounted by the fall of my horse, I was greatly shocked at witnessing an act of wanton cruelty which it was not in my power to prevent. A man of Griffith's troop rode up to a French dragoon who was lying wounded on the ground, and at his approach raised himself with difficulty to beg for mercy, stripping off his cross-belts at the same time to show that he surrendered. I hallooed to the fellow to spare him, but before I could reach the spot the villain had split the Frenchman's skull with a blow of his sabre, and galloped away. It was fortunate for him that he got out of my reach, for, in the indignation I felt at his conduct, I should certainly have treated him in the same manner. I heard afterwards that the excuse he offered for this dastardly conduct, when twitted by his comrades, was that he did not like " to let the day pass without cutting down a Frenchman, and could not suffer such a favourable opportunity to slip !"

It was also reported that several of the French who were wounded and had received quarter, fired at our men as soon as their backs were turned, and of course paid the forfeit of this treachery with their lives.

After running three or four hundred yards, I met some men of my troop leading captured French horses, from which I selected one to replace my lost charger. Several straggling Frenchmen passed close beside me, whilst I was on foot, without offering me the slightest molestation; they probably took me for one of their own people, or were too intent on providing for their own safety to think of any other object. The animal I selected was a bad goer and very ill-broke; it had belonged to a quartermaster or subaltern officer, and was handsomely caparisoned, but the saddle was far from comfortable, and the stirrups so long that I could scarcely reach them with the point of my toe. This horse was such a headstrong beast that he was near placing me in an awkward predicament. In the act of leading the men I had collected against the squadron of Chasseurs which had escaped from

Lord Paget, I leaped over a ditch which lay between the two bodies; and when the attack was countermanded, I suppose my steed recognized his old companions, as the enemy was then passing at the distance of little more than a hundred yards, and I had the greatest difficulty in forcing him to recross the ditch, and for some time expected to be carried into the midst of the French squadron in spite of all my exertions to the contrary.

When I was remounted, I saw that the squadron was so far advanced I had no chance of overtaking it. I therefore employed myself in collecting the prisoners we had taken, whom I sent to the rear under an escort. They seemed very much terrified, having, as I understood, been taught to expect no quarter would be given them; and when I assured them they had no cause for apprehension of that sort, they kissed my hands, embraced my knees, and committed all manner of extravagancies. Many of these men were Germans and remarkably fine-looking fellows.

I had now collected about thirty hussars— including those who had been sent back with the prisoners, and whose horses had been unable to keep up with the rest—when the Tenth appeared on an eminence near the scene of action, and were supposed to belong to the enemy. As soon as I noticed this fresh body of cavalry, I looked anxiously round the plain in hopes of discovering a rallying point; but the regiment was so completely scattered in pursuit that I could not perceive a single squadron formed on the field, and our situation appeared so desperate that I considered the only thing that remained for us to do was to sell our lives as dearly as possible. I therefore determined to lead my small division against the body of Chasseurs which had escaped from Lord Paget; but I had scarcely given the word to advance, when his lordship, who as well as every other officer had been deceived by the appearance of the Tenth in a quarter where they were not expected, ordered the "rally" to be sounded, and Colonel Grant, who had just arrived at the spot and approved of my design, said the signal must be immediately obeyed. I was thus reluctantly obliged to abandon the meditated attack, which, from our relative positions, would in all probability have been attended with complete success, as we had an opportunity of charging on the enemy's flank.

I was happy to exchange the French horse for my own mare, which was brought to me soon after the regiment had reassembled, having been found in the custody of some men of the Tenth, but I was not so fortunate as to recover the valise with my baggage, which was strapped to the saddle at the time I lost her.

We learned from the prisoners that their force consisted of the 8th Regiment of Dragoons and a provisional regiment of *chasseurs à cheval*, commanded by the General of Brigade, Debelle, whose horses and baggage fell into our hands. It appeared by the returns found in his portfolio that the French had about eight hundred men mounted in the field, whilst we only mustered betwixt three and four hundred, as, independent of various small detachments, above a hundred men and horses were left at Melgar de Abaxo. Although but few of the enemy were killed on the spot, a great proportion of the prisoners were severely wounded, chiefly by the sabre ; their total loss exceeded 300 men, for a number of their wounded who, after escaping from the field had been left on the road from inability to proceed, were secured and brought to headquarters by our

15

infantry, who afterwards occupied the villages where they had taken shelter.

Colonel Dud'huit and twelve officers of the 8th Dragoons were taken. This regiment, which was in the front, bore the brunt of the attack, and suffered most severely. Colonel Dugens, three officers, and about a hundred of the Chasseurs, were made prisoners. We understood that the Eighth was a favourite corps; it had served in all the late campaigns, and gained great credit at Marengo, Austerlitz, Jena, Eylau, and Friedland; several of the officers wore the Cross of the Legion of Honour; and several of the sergeants and privates bore honorary badges. The clothing and appointments, both of men and horses, were strong and serviceable; and the brass helmets, in point of utility and martial appearance, might be substituted with advantage in our Service for the cocked hat of the heavy dragoon. The French officers expressed surprise at our temerity in attacking them, and at their own defeat. At first they took us for Spaniards, and expected an easy victory. It is but doing them justice to remark that they received our charge with the most determined firmness, but after their ranks were once broken they made no effort to retrieve the day, but appeared panic-struck, and only intent on making their escape.

Colonel Tascher, nephew to the Empress Josephine, commanded the Chasseurs, but we could not ascertain whether he was present in the action. The French were better mounted than we had been led to expect from the report of some of our officers who had been on service with the regiment in the campaigns of 1794 and 1799. None of their horses were under fourteen hands and a half, and several were taken into our brigade to replace such as had become unfit for service. They were in pretty good condition, but most of their backs were galled ; this was not surprising, as they had only arrived at Sahagun a few days before, having made almost daily marches since the beginning of October, when they left Hanover ; and the French dragoons take very little care of their horses.

There was not a single man of the Fifteenth killed in the field ;* we had about thirty wounded, five or six severely, two of whom died the next

* The actual losses were, four men died of wounds, two officers and nineteen other ranks wounded ; four horses killed, four wounded, and ten missing.—Ed.

day; most of the others were so slightly hurt
that they returned to their duty within a week.
I expected the French would have displayed
more skill in the use of the sabre than our men,
but the fact proved quite the reverse, for notwithstanding their swords were considerably
longer, they had no chance with us. Our hussars
obtained a good deal of plunder, as the prisoners
were well supplied with many trinkets and ingots
of silver, the produce of plate stolen from the
churches and houses of the Spaniards, and melted
to render it more portable. Many of their valises
contained fans and parasols—rather extraordinary
articles of equipment for a winter campaign.
General Debelle lost his baggage and horses; we
also got possession of the papers belonging to
the staff of the brigade, and the seals of the
8th Regiment, besides a great number of private
letters which were scattered about the fields
of the captors without any regard to the tender
nature of the contents.

Although the success of the action was rendered
incomplete, owing to the very extraordinary conduct of General Slade and some mistakes of Lord
Paget, it nevertheless impressed such an idea of
the superiority of our cavalry on the mind of the

enemy as induced them to avoid as much as possible coming in contact with us. Indeed, I can only attribute the want of enterprise displayed by them on many subsequent occasions, when, owing to their immense superiority in point of numbers and the inefficient state of our horses, they had favourable opportunities of destroying the regiment, to the lessons they had received at Sahagun, Rueda, Valencia, etc.

If General Slade had sent forward an officer to announce his approach, or if he had joined in the pursuit, in all probability not a single Frenchman would have escaped. The whole affair did not occupy an hour, and the regiment remained drawn up under the walls of the town, without any refreshment, from seven in the morning till five in the afternoon ; whilst the Tenth, who had no share in the dangers of the day, were sent into quarters before us.

About three o'clock an alarm was caused by the appearance of a considerable body of troops on the Mayorga road ; the regiment was immediately mounted and formed in line, and the Tenth were ordered to turn out. But on the return of the aide-de-camp who was sent to reconnoitre, this supposed enemy proved to be

16

a division of our own infantry, which entered the
town soon after.

We were all sufficiently tired of our situation
and the view of the walls of Sahagun, and when
we were at length permitted to take up our
quarters our first care was to make the best
preparations for dinner that circumstances would
allow.   After enjoying the luxury of devoting an
hour to the duties of the toilet, which had been
but irregularly performed of late, I was preparing
to make a vigorous attack upon some beef broth
and a Spanish *olla*, when I was interrupted by
the appearance of an orderly sergeant with the
unwelcome intelligence that I was ordered on
duty, and that the picquets were already assembled and waiting for me.   It was extremely
mortifying to be obliged to leave my dinner
untasted, but as there was no remedy, I was
forced to comfort myself with the hope of being
attached to the inlying picquet ; in this, however,
I was disappointed, being sent with an officer
and eighty men to occupy Nuestra Senora de la
Puente, at the distance of half a league from
Sahagun, on the road to Carrion de los Condes.
It was quite dark before we reached our destination, which rendered it impossible to make any

observations on the directions of the roads or
nature of the ground in the vicinity of our
position; therefore, after posting vedettes and
despatching the necessary patrols, Lieutenant
Jebb and myself took possession of the apartment assigned for our use. It was a large room
without furniture, excepting a wooden bench;
there was a scanty fire on the hearth; and the
wintry blast had unrestrained entrance from
every quarter. Our endeavours to procure any
sort of provisions in this miserable place were
fruitless, the inhabitants assuring us that they
had not even a supper for themselves. I had
already fasted twenty-four hours, and the prospect
of remaining several hours longer without food
was by no means exhilarating. The officer of
the Tenth who was with me seemed to have
fared almost as ill as myself, and a small quantity
of chocolate which I found in a corner of my
haversack proved very acceptable, in the absence
of all other nourishment, previous to composing
ourselves on the wooden bench, which was the
substitute for a bed.

I passed a very anxious night, for I was aware
that the enemy was in considerable force at
Saldana and Carrion, and, owing to the circum-

stances already mentioned, we were necessarily
ignorant of the *carte du pays*, with which the
French, on the other hand, were perfectly acquainted, from having occupied this part of the
province for some days.   These considerations,
which received additional force from the darkness
of the night, and a heavy drifting snow, made
me apprehensive of being surprised, which, in our
situation, might have compromised the safety of
the army.   To add to the difficulties of our position, above fifty of the horses were crowded into
a long narrow hall, which served for a stable ;
the entrance and passage were barely wide enough
to admit the animals singly ; a long time was
therefore required to get them out again, and in
the event of any confusion arising in the attempt
to turn out in a hurry, all egress would have
become impossible.   The remaining horses, which
could not be accommodated in this hall, were
sheltered under a piazza that supported the front
of the building, and were subjected to the same
disadvantages in a less degree.   If the weather
had been moderate, I should have preferred
bivouacking to the risk of suffering the men and
horses to be cooped up in such an inconvenient
place ; but the intense cold and heavy snow made

me unwilling to expose the troops, unless there
had existed an absolute necessity for such a
measure.

About midnight I rode out to visit the different
patrols, and with difficulty found my way back
to our post. Soon after my return we were
alarmed by the report of a carbine, followed by
the clattering of hoofs on the pavement under
the windows of our chamber. This noise was
occasioned by one of our vedettes who had
galloped in to give notice of the approach of a
body of cavalry, whom he concluded to be
enemies as they did not answer his challenge.
I ordered the picquet to turn out as fast as possible, but I had scarcely collected a dozen mounted
men, with whom I hastened to occupy the approach to the bridge, when the party which had
caused the alarm appeared in sight, and proved
to be a patrol of the 7th Hussars, who had
missed their way owing to the darkness of the
night.

22nd.—At length the morning dawned, to my
great joy, although it was ushered in by a thick
fog and a heavy fall of snow. As the day advanced I began to think we were forgotten by
our friends at headquarters, and therefore sent

a quartermaster to Sahagun to inquire when we might expect to be relieved, and to procure rations for the men and forage for the horses. I then rode out to reconnoitre the adjacent country, and afterwards took a survey of our comfortless quarters.

The place where we were stationed was a farmhouse, adjoining a Romerio, a place to which pilgrimages are made, which abuts upon a bridge across the Cea. It contains a miraculous image of the Virgin, called " Our Lady of the Bridge " and highly celebrated in the neighbouring districts, but whose efforts in the defence of Sahagun have not proved so efficacious as the interposition of " Our Lady of the Pillar " at Zaragoza. The shrine, however, was shown to me by a woman, who seemed to have the care of the chapel, with many high eulogiums of Nuestra Senora de la Puente, and earnest assurances of the blessings experienced by the neighbourhood from her presence.

The house is tenanted by a shepherd's family, with his assistants ; it is spacious, and contains a suite of large rooms, fitted up in a superior style to the rest of the building. These apartments are embellished with allegorical paintings and representations of portions of sacred history, and I understood from my cicerone that the ecclesiastics of the province assembled here at certain periods, but I could not make out for what purpose, except to eat a good dinner in the hall which served as a stable for our horses.   In exploring the premises I opened a door which led into a garret where the family slept, and discovered the uniform and part of the accoutrements of one of the French dragoons, still wet with blood.   Adjoining the house are extensive courtyards, surrounded by low sheds capable of containing several hundred sheep.   The shepherds, who are obliged to brave the elements in the most severe weather, wear dresses of sheepskins with the wool outwards, which gives them a most savage and uncouth appearance.   They are attended by large dogs of great strength and courage to protect the flocks from wolves, which come down from the mountains in great numbers. One of these dogs attached himself to the regiment whilst we were in their district, and followed us to England.

When the quartermaster returned, he informed me that the Fifteenth had moved to a village one league in advance; that we were to remain at our post until further orders ; and that forage and provisions would be sent to us in the afternoon. This intelligence was far from agreeable, as it held out the prospect of passing another night in our present quarters ; but at five o'clock I received orders to return to Sahagun with the picquet, and then to join my regiment at Villa Peschenel, where we arrived at seven o'clock in a violent storm of wind and rain. I went immediately to Colonel Grant's quarters to report our arrival, and found a number of officers at dinner with him. As I had been almost fifty hours without food, the sight of a well-furnished table could not fail to give me satisfaction, and I did not require twice bidding to join the party. When I retired to my own quarters I had the pleasure of meeting my friend Baron During, who had rejoined the regiment the day before.

CHAPTER IV

[*MOORE'S infantry occupied Sahagun on the day of the cavalry action, and here a halt was called, the British commander proposing to move forward on the night of the 23rd to Carrion, for the purpose of attacking Soult at daybreak on the 25th at Saldana. Romana was to have co-operated by moving 10,000 of his Spaniards to Mansilla. The British troops were actually on parade on the evening of the 23rd, preparing, in high spirits, for the advance, when they were directed to stand fast, Sir John Moore having heard that the French were on the march northward from Madrid, and that Napoleon himself was well on his way to Benevente. The orders already given for the forward movement were now at once countermanded, and the arrangements for the retreat were made, Moore meaning to fall back upon Astorga in the hope of being able there to make a stand with the assistance of Romana's troops. The British cavalry demonstrated towards Carrion and Saldana, while the infantry divisions fell back by*

*Valencia and Valderas, the retreat commencing on
December 24.*

*On the 26th the main body of the British was at
Benevente, and already many scenes of disorder had
been witnessed; on the night of the 28th the Ezla
was crossed, and on the 29th the British divisions
were at Astorga, La Baneza, and at Acebes, while
on the 30th the main body was concentrated at
Astorga.   Here Moore had no more than two days'
supplies to carry him the fifty miles to Villafranca;
he was clear of Astorga on the last day of the year,
and on January 1 Napoleon entered the town, to find
the British cavalry had only left that morning, and
that Moore had escaped him.   Here he handed over
further pursuit to Soult, Bessières, and Ney, returning himself to France.*

*From Astorga two brigades, those of Craufurd and
Alten, marched by Orense on Vigo, covering Moore's
left flank, the rest of the army falling back on
Corunna.   The main body under Moore reached
Bembibere on December 31, Villafranca on January 1,
halted the 2nd, and was at Herrerias on the 3rd.*

*The work of the cavalry during these memorable,
and, for that arm, " golden" days, is fully described
by Captain Gordon.*]

December 23rd.—There having been a complete thaw yesterday, and heavy rain from five

o'clock in the evening until ten, after which the
frost returned with increased severity, the roads
were in consequence covered with ice, which
made riding dangerous, as it was scarcely possible
to keep the horses on their legs.

Sir John Moore had received information*
that Marshal Soult was posted with eighteen
thousand men at Saldana, a small town six
leagues from Sahagun, and determined to attack
his position, the Marquis de la Romana having
engaged to support him with ten or twelve
thousand Spaniards. The army was accordingly
ordered to move in two columns upon Carrion ;
the Fifteenth turned out at five o'clock in the
evening, and marched with the left column to
St. Nicholas,† three leagues from our quarters at
Villa Peschenel. We arrived there at eight
o'clock, and after passing through the village the
cavalry and horse artillery were formed and dis-

* See Appendix IV.

† In De la Borde's map of the roads in Leon, Cisueros is
marked about halfway betwixt Sahagun and Carrion, and I
think it most probable that this is the proper name of the
village to which we marched on the evening of December 23,
when the army moved forward to attack Marshal Soult, and
which is called St. Nicholas in our orderly books, where the
Spanish names of places were often strangely metamorphosed.

mounted on a ridge of land, where we remained until midnight. The cold was most intense, and the ground covered with snow, circumstances which did not tend to reconcile us to the delay at this place, especially when whispers began to circulate a report—which proved too well founded—that the intention of advancing was abandoned. During this interval many of the hussars, who had been much harassed of late by incessant duty, laid down beside their horses to gain a little repose. I made myself a very comfortable bed by spreading a truss of hay on the frozen snow, from which I was roused by the order for the regiment to mount and return to our former quarters; but the left squadron halted at Villa Lebrin, halfway betwixt St. Nicholas and Sahagun.

It had been Sir John Moore's intention to make a night march to Carrion, force the bridge there, and attack the enemy at Saldana the next day; but this plan was relinquished in consequence of most unwelcome intelligence received at headquarters after the columns were put in motion. The despatches stated that all the corps of the French army in the Peninsula had been ordered to move on Leon; that Bonaparte was advancing from Madrid by forced marches at the head of 80,000 men in order to cut off our communications with Galicia; and it was reported that Soult, having received considerable reinforcements, had advanced from Saldana to Carrion, where he had taken up a strong position. The Commander of the Forces was also disappointed of the assistance promised him by the Marquis de la Romana, who, instead of co-operating with 10,000 men, could only bring 7,000 into the field, with whom he arrived at Mansilla de las Mulas, six leagues from Sahagun, on the afternoon of the 23rd; and little or no dependence could be placed on these troops, as they were in a very inefficient state of discipline and equipment.

In this situation of affairs a speedy retreat appeared to be the only measure that offered a probable chance of preserving the army from destruction; but the mode in which this retreat was conducted makes it questionable whether we could have suffered greater losses if the attack on Soult had been persisted in, and followed up by a dash on Madrid, or an attempt made to join the Aragonese and Catalonians, amongst whom the spirit of resistance to the invaders was still active.

17

Sir John Moore having determined to fall back on Galicia, the retreat commenced on the 24th, and, had it been delayed forty-eight hours, the enemy would have reached the Ezla before us, in which case we could have had no choice but death or surrender.

24th.—The Squadron remained at Villa Lebrin, keeping a strong picquet in advance and patrolling some miles on the road to Carrion. The owner of the house we occupied was an old man whom they called Don Pedro ; his establishment was composed of an old woman, a cow, and an ass— at least these were the only animals we discovered on the premises. When our host was questioned as to his profession and employment, he answered that he was a philosopher and passed his time in study. As it seemed rather an extraordinary circumstance to meet with a philosopher by profession in such an obscure situation, I inquired minutely into the nature of his studies, when he declared himself to be conversant with all the sciences, but particularly attached to astronomy. He boasted much of his library, which he kept carefully locked up, although I found it only contained from twenty to thirty small volumes, chiefly treatises on divinity and the legends of the Roman Catholic Church. I must, however, do Don Pedro the justice to allow that the apathy with which he contemplated the miseries that threatened his native country might be considered a sufficient proof of his claim to the title of philosopher in one sense of the term.

The atmosphere was as gloomy as our prospects, and we passed the day without any communication with the rest of the army. All remained quiet in our front, and we could get no information of the enemy's movements or intentions.

In the houses of the peasants in this district a sort of shelf is built over the hearth in the kitchens, similar to the flue in a hothouse, but broader. It is customary for the servants to sleep on this shelf in winter on account of the warmth. I made a trial of it, and found it an exceeding hot berth.

25th.—In the course of the morning a number of suspicious-looking people, who could not give satisfactory accounts of themselves, were seized at our advanced posts, and forwarded to the headquarters. They represented themselves to be Portuguese, who had followed the army from Portugal; but we did not understand their language sufficiently to discover whether they spoke the truth or not. About four o'clock in the afternoon orders were received for the squadron to repair to Sahagun, and we turned out immediately, leaving a fine turkey and a piece of beef which had been provided for our Christmas dinner. A picquet was left in the village under the command of Baron During, who remained there until nine o'clock the next morning, when the different picquets were united to form the rear-guard of the cavalry. On our road to Sahagun we passed over the ground where the action of the 21st took place, and I observed several corpses unburied, " a prey to dogs and birds." The peasants had stripped them, and it was reported that the body of a female was found amongst the number. The French entered the town on the 26th, and doubtless took ample revenge on the inhabitants for the indignities offered to the remains of their fallen comrades.

We arrived at Sahagun just in time to join the mess, where all the officers of the regiment, except those absent on duty, were assembled to celebrate the day ; but the mirth and jollity usually prevalent at this season were considerably damped by reflection on the critical situation in which we were placed.

Lieutenant Penrice was dangerously ill of typhus fever, and as there was no proper mode of conveyance for him, even if it had been judged advisable to remove him, he was committed to the care of a Spanish physician, with whom Lord Paget left a letter addressed to the commanding officer of any French troops which might enter the town, requesting kind treatment for Penrice, and offering, in the event of his recovery, to give any officer of the same rank taken prisoner on the 21st in exchange for him.*

26th.—The brigade assembled at six o'clock, and was ordered to proceed to Valderas, nine leagues from Sahagun. On approaching Mayorga we found that town occupied by the enemy, and learned that the baggage of the cavalry, which had been sent forward the day before, was captured by them. Lord Paget immediately pushed on with the Tenth, followed by the Fifteenth. Our left squadron was ordered to support the troop of horse artillery attached to the brigade, and the rattling of the guns as we galloped through the streets completed the panic of the

* This officer recovered and returned to England.—Ed.

18

inhabitants, who were making the most doleful lamentations. When we had got clear of the town, two squadrons of *chasseurs à cheval* were discovered, formed on a rising ground about a mile distant. Lord Paget directed General Slade to attack them with a squadron of the Tenth, supported by the remainder of the regiment. The General moved off at a trot, but had not advanced far when he halted to have some alteration made in the length of his stirrups. An aide-de-camp was sent to inquire the cause of this delay, and the squadron was again put in motion ; but the General's stirrups were not yet adjusted to his mind, and he halted again before they had advanced a hundred yards.

Lord Paget, whose patience was by this time quite exhausted, then ordered Colonel Leigh to take the lead. The Tenth charged gallantly, routed the enemy, and took between forty and fifty prisoners, with little loss on their part.

It is extraordinary that the French should have awaited this attack, as, from their commanding position, they must have been aware of the disparity of numbers, which precluded them from any chance of success ; and if they had been inclined to avoid an action, it would have been impossible for us to have overtaken them. Owing to the delay this rencontre occasioned, it was almost dark when we reached Valderas, and, as the place was full of troops, we had great difficulty in finding quarters for the men and horses. I was sent soon afterwards to take command of a picquet posted on the Mayorga road, about half a mile from the town.

On this occasion a circumstance came under my observation which marked the very negligent manner in which the duty of the general staff was performed at a period when the army was certainly in great jeopardy, as strong corps of the enemy were closing round us on every side, and a night attack on our quarters was by no means an impossible event. I had received instructions to be particularly vigilant, to keep up a constant communication with the other picquets, and to patrol the roads leading to Mayorga and Sahagun; and I was assured that a party of artillery, with a howitzer, would be attached to my picquet to protect the bridge across the Cea.

This party, however, did not make its appearance, and it was near midnight before I received the countersign. The night passed away without any serious alarm, although from the reports brought in hourly by the patrols we had reason to suppose the enemy could not be very far distant.

27*th.*—A very thick fog came on at daybreak, which made it impossible to discern objects at the distance of a horse's length. The church bells sounded for a long time to give notice of a fire which had broken out in the town ; it burned with great fury, and caused considerable damage before it was extinguished.

Here we began to shoot the horses and mules which were lame, or in other respects unfit for hard work. I counted about forty lying dead in the streets of this place ; and, at a subsequent period of the retreat, ten of these animals were destroyed, on a moderate computation, for every mile we marched.

The troops — cavalry and horse artillery — quitted Valderas at nine o'clock ; the picquets were called in soon after, and formed the rear-guard. Colonel Grant was detached early in the morning with a squadron of the Fifteenth to make a reconnaissance in the direction of Villalpando ; he rejoined our column in the afternoon without having gained any intelligence of the enemy. Owing to a thaw which had come on since the 24th, and the number of troops and heavy carriages that had already passed, the roads were extremely heavy, and in some places the artillery horses were scarcely able to drag the guns through the sloughs. Our route lay through several villages, which exhibited melancholy proofs of the shameful devastation committed by the infantry which had preceded us; we observed one in flames whilst we were at a considerable distance, and it was still burning when we passed through it. The inhabitants shouted, "Vivan los Franceses," and we overtook some stragglers who had been stripped and maltreated by the Spaniards.

We crossed the Ezla about five o'clock, leaving a picquet on the right bank of the river near the bridge, and the Seventh, Tenth, and Eighteenth, with the horse artillery, proceeded to Benevente. The Hussars of the German Legion, I believe, remained with the picquet. The Fifteenth was detached to San Christoval, a small village on the right bank of the Ezla, where we found good quarters and plenty of forage. Our day's march was seven leagues.

28th.—At ten o'clock in the morning, whilst

the men were busily employed in foraging, the
bugles sounded "To horse!" and we turned out
in a great hurry, in consequence of a report that
the French had forced the bridge ; this, however,
proved a false alarm, and the regiment was sent
back to quarters, with the exception of the left
squadron, which was detached to destroy the
ferry-boats on the river between San Christoval
and Valencia. The ferry at Villalfer, two leagues
from the former village, is on the left bank of
the river ; the boat happening to be on our
side taking in passengers, a party was immediately set to work upon it, but, being unprovided
with proper tools for the purpose, it cost a great
deal of time and labour to render it unserviceable. Detachments were sent to destroy the
boats at the other ferries, and, after posting
vedettes to watch the village, we marched about
a league farther, to Villa Guexida, where we
considered ourselves in perfect security, as the
Spaniards had assured us that the river was not
fordable.

We had a false alarm at four o'clock, occasioned by a drove of oxen, which, owing to the
hazy state of the weather, was mistaken for a
troop of cavalry until we were undeceived by

a nearer view; and at six o'clock the vedettes, stationed at the ferry, sent us information that a strong division of the enemy's troops had entered the village, broke open the houses, and commenced a general massacre of the pigs and poultry, without paying the slightest attention to the remonstrances and lamentations of the owners. They rode into the Ezla to water their horses, and abused our men in broken English. Soon after their arrival a number of loaded mules, driven by Spaniards, forded the river a short distance below the ferry.

In consequence of this disagreeable intelligence, we moved from Villa Guexida at eight o'clock and occupied Simones, a small village about a mile below Villalfer. A picquet was stationed to watch the ford; the remainder of the squadron, after two hours' repose, was drawn up in the plain until daylight, when we withdrew into the village, and remained mounted until eight o'clock. The men were then sent into quarters.

29th.—After breakfast Major Leitch and myself ascended the tower of the church, from whence we could plainly distinguish the enemy without a glass. Their force, composed of

cavalry, infantry, and artillery, amounted — as
we learnt afterwards—to nearly three thousand
men. At ten o'clock they pointed two guns at
our advanced picquet, which was in consequence
withdrawn into the village; and shortly after
this we received orders to follow the regiment,
which had marched to the bridge at Castro
Gonzalo, to support the rest of our cavalry, who
were engaged with the French.

We turned out in a few minutes, and proceeded towards the scene of action as fast as the
horses could trot; but before we reached San
Christoval we received directions to halt and
wait for the regiment, which soon came up to
us, and the whole body marched to the Villa
Guexida, where we halted three hours, and at
five o'clock continued our route to Puente de la
Bisana. Lieutenant Hancox was left behind in
command of a small picquet, with instructions to
watch the enemy's motions during the night, and
to follow the regiment at break of day. The
division of the French army at Villalfer crossed
the river before this party withdrew from Villa
Guexida. Major Leitch was detached with a
strong picquet to patrol the bank of the river as
far as Villa Manana, with orders to occupy that

village during the night, and to rejoin the brigade at La Baneza. It is surprising this detachment was not intercepted by one of the numerous corps which crossed the Ezla at different points, and overspread the whole district within a few hours after Lord Paget's division quitted Benevente. It was fortunate for us that the enemy contented themselves with occupying Villalfer on the 28th and 29th, as they were in sufficient force to have destroyed the Fifteenth, which was entirely unsupported on both those days.

I had an opportunity of conversing with several officers and men who had been engaged in the action near Benevente, and the account which follows is the substance of the information thus collected.

It having been determined to destroy the bridge over the Ezla in order to impede the enemy's progress, a party of Engineers was employed in mining it when we crossed on the 27th, and it was blown up the next night. General Lefebvre arrived at Castro Gonzalo on the morning of the 29th with seven squadrons of the Hussars of the Imperial Guard, and found the bridge impassable; but observing only a

small picquet in the plain he conceived it would
be an easy conquest, as he concluded our army
had evacuated Benevente. A ford was soon
discovered, by which he crossed the river, and
attacked the picquet, composed of about a
hundred men of the Eighteenth and Third
German Hussars; these were, however, quickly
joined by the inlying picquet, and succeeded in
keeping the French at bay until the whole of
the cavalry and horse artillery were assembled,
and hurrying to the scene of action. On the
approach of this strong reinforcement the enemy
recrossed the Ezla, and formed in good order on
the opposite bank, where they remained until
the arrival of our artillery, a few rounds from
which drove them over the hill in confusion.

The gallantry of our troops was most conspicuous in this affair, as there were not above
two hundred and fifty British, actually, opposed
to six or seven hundred French; but our loss
was proportionately severe. The Eighteenth
and German Hussars, who bore the brunt of
the engagement, had sixty or seventy killed and
wounded; the loss of the enemy was about
thirty killed and seventy made prisoners. Only
three privates of the Fifteenth were present, one

of whom was shot through the heart. General Lefebvre was amongst the prisoners. Upon the repulse of his troops he attempted to ford the river, but his horse being unable to stem the current, he was obliged to return to the shore, when he was attacked by a private of the Tenth, to whom he surrendered after receiving a slight wound.

It was known that Bonaparte slept at Villalpando, which is only five leagues from Benevente, on December 28, and it may be presumed that he suffered a severe mortification at the defeat sustained by the Hussars of his Guard almost within his own view.

The Eighteenth have been uniformly successful in their rencontres with the enemy. During the advance of the army—on their route from Valderas to Sahagun—thirty men of that regiment fell in at Valencia de Don Juan with a hundred French dragoons, whom they attacked without hesitation, and put to flight, with a loss of twenty killed and taken prisoners. But the Hussars of the Guard were superior in every respect to any of the troops with whom we had been engaged hitherto. Their dress and appointments were showy and at the same time serviceable, and they displayed the most perfect discipline and determined valour.

The Seventh, Tenth, Eighteenth, and German Hussars marched from Benevente in the afternoon, and the Fifteenth joined them at the Puente de la Bisana, three leagues from La Baneza. Before the army left Benevente immense magazines of stores of every description were burned, and several thousand pairs of shoes were destroyed or given to the Spaniards, at the very time when a great proportion of our infantry was but ill-provided with that important article of equipment.

30*th*.—We reached La Baneza at eight o'clock after a very cold and uncomfortable night march, in the course of which we halted for three hours at Puente de la Bisana, where the Engineers were making preparations to blow up the bridge; but the attempt proved abortive.

As soon as the dawn enabled us to distinguish the objects by which we were surrounded, I observed that the road was strewed with the empty canisters, cartridge paper, wadding, etc., of ammunition, that had been destroyed to prevent it from falling into the enemy's hands. Several horses and mules were shot during this

march, and the road was often obstructed by
their carcasses; interruptions were also occasioned
at intervals by the smoking remains of caissons
and carriages, which had been burned when the
means of transport failed.

For some days past our horses had begun to
knock up, owing to the harassing duty on which
they had been employed without intermission,
the deficiencies of proper forage, and, above all,
to the want of shoes.   The forge-carts, with the
tools and iron, were burned or left behind on the
27th by order of the Commander of the Forces,
because they could not keep up with the rest
of the baggage; but if the farriers had been
furnished with everything they required, the
regiment never had a sufficient respite from
duty to allow time to get the horses properly
shod.

31*st*.—The brigade assembled soon after midnight, and marched from La Baneza at one
o'clock, leaving several houses on fire.   Within
half a league of Astorga we found a picquet
of the Light Battalion of the German Legion,
stationed in a village that was nearly reduced
to ashes.   The officers told us that the Spanish
army, estimated at 120,000 men, was in can-

19

tonments in the town and adjacent villages, and that it was determined our combined forces should await the arrival of the French army, and give it battle in the plain. It is difficult to conjecture how such an absurd report could have originated or obtained credit; the town was, in fact, occupied by the Marquis de la Romana's corps, in consequence of which we found it difficult to get quarters. This Spanish force amounted to about 6,000 men in the most deplorable condition. They were all ill-clothed; many were without shoes, and even without arms; a pestilential fever raged amongst them; they had been without bread for several days, and were quite destitute of money. In short, their state could not be more justly described than in that French bulletin which, alluding to Romana's army, says: "These miserable wretches fill every hospital." Miserable indeed they were, and almost every house in Astorga contained some of their dead or dying.

We had been very irregularly furnished with provisions for some days; the troops received meat here and flour instead of bread, but neither wine nor spirits. During the retreat the army was seldom supplied with rations above once in three days, and the cavalry were sometimes four or five days together without getting any. The officers were frequently as ill-provided for as the men, but Baron During, who messed with me, was an excellent forager, and we were generally able to supply some of our less provident comrades.

There was a false alarm at two o'clock, when the Spanish troops assembled in the plaza, and in the evening one of their picquets came into the courtyard of the house we occupied, to warm themselves at a large fire which our hussars had made. I spoke to some of the men, who were evidently suffering from famine and disease; they declared they had eaten nothing for three days, and when we gave them the remains of our dinner, and money to buy wine, their expressions of gratitude were unbounded.

There was another false alarm at eight o'clock, when the whole of the cavalry turned out and remained at the alarm-post until eleven, at which hour we followed the Reserve under General Paget. The ground was still covered with snow, and the frost was most intense. In the course of the night we passed Romana's army, which we now saw for the last time; their march was directed on Orense by Ponteferrado, but the train of artillery, consisting of forty fine pieces, kept the great road to Corunna.

Astorga was the point at which the different corps of the French army met, and the force assembled there amounted to sixty or seventy thousand men. Bonaparte arrived on New Year's Day; and having failed in the attempt to intercept the British before they reached the mountain passes of Galicia, after reviewing his troops, he committed the charge of the pursuit to Marshals Soult and Ney with three divisions, and returned himself to Madrid.

January 1st, 1809. — If our Christmas was gloomy, the New Year did not afford us brighter prospects. On the contrary, our situation was become even more critical, and it was difficult to controvert the reasoning of those amongst us who predicted that this month would witness the capture or destruction of one of the finest armies that ever left the shores of Britain. Our difficulties and distresses increased at every league we marched, and the disorganization of the troops became more apparent every day.

Early in the morning we overtook a number of waggons loaded with the cotton which was taken at Rueda by the Eighteenth ; we also passed several cars filled with the sick and wounded belonging to our army. Owing to the deep snow and the dreadful state of the roads, these carriages made very little progress, and were all taken by the enemy before night. The road was occasionally crowded with coaches, calashes, and litters, containing Spanish families, who were endeavouring to reach Corunna and Ferrol, where they expected to be in safety from the hostile army. In the afternoon we passed through a large village of the Mauregatos, which had been completely destroyed by fire. The wretched inhabitants were sitting amidst the trifling articles of property they had been able to save from the flames, contemplating the ruins of their houses in silent despair. The bodies of several Spaniards who had died of hunger or disease, or perished from the inclemency of the weather, were lying scattered around, and heightened the horrors of the scene. The village had been burned by some of our infantry, and scarcely an hour passed in which we did not witness the most pitiable misery, occasioned by the excesses of our troops, which it was impossible to prevent. Numbers continually straggled to the

20

villages near the road, which, after pillaging, they generally set on fire ; and whenever they discovered the places where wine was concealed, they drank until they incapacitated themselves from rejoining the line of march, or perished in the flames they had kindled. It is not surprising that this conduct excited in the breasts of the natives a detestation of the British, which induced them to retaliate, as often as they had the opportunity, by murdering or ill-treating the stragglers.

The only apology to be offered for the soldiers is that they were certainly not treated like friends by the Spaniards, who, although they saw us fainting for want of food, secreted their provisions, and pretended to be unable to supply our necessities, even when the most ample payment was tendered. Whilst I am upon this subject, I must do the dragoons the justice to declare that it was but seldom they committed any depredations on the property of the inhabitants, neither were they guilty of the wanton excesses in which the foot-soldiers appeared to take delight. In fact, discipline and subordination were preserved in the cavalry regiments, when no remains of either could be traced in the conduct of the rest of the army. This censure, however, does not apply to the Artillery, the brigade of Guards, and the Twentieth, Forty-third, Fifty-second, Ninety-fifth, and Light Battalions of the German Legion, which formed the reserve; the behaviour of these corps was on all occasions praiseworthy.

We reached Bembibere about four o'clock, and found the town occupied by some regiments of infantry and cavalry. The Fifteenth was therefore detached to Mansanassa, a small village half a league distant on the road to Ponteferrado, where we enjoyed a few hours' rest after three successive night marches. Our left squadron had been constantly on duty since the morning of the 28th, and the horses had not been un-saddled during that period.

It was near five o'clock before we got into quarters, and soon after midnight the "rouse" was sounded. On repairing to the alarm-post we learned that the picquets of the Seventh and Tenth had been driven into Bembibere, but as the enemy had retired we were sent back to our quarters. Several of our officers were billeted in the house of the priest of the parish, where I observed a method of keeping fruit for winter

use which was new to me. The padre's family
occupied a large room which served both for
parlour and dormitory, as there were four or five
beds in it; and from the ceiling of this chamber
many bunches of grapes and a great number of
apples were suspended singly by threads. The
reverend gentleman was very niggardly, and
positively refused to let us taste his fruit; we
therefore took the liberty of helping ourselves in
defiance of his threats, and found the flavour uncommonly fine. The grapes were particularly
luscious.

2nd. — The regiment reassembled at four
o'clock, and joined the division at Bembibere,
where a party was employed in burning a quantity of officers' baggage and regimental stores.
We remained there above two hours waiting for
orders, and in that interval Captain Cochrane
was detached with the old picquet to make a
reconnaissance on the Astorga road, for the purpose of ascertaining the strength and position of
the troops which had disturbed us during the
night. This party rejoined us shortly after we
commenced our march, having been forced to
retire before a regiment of *chasseurs à cheval,*
which they fell in with about a league from

Bembibere.   Captain Cochrane, upon making
this report of his proceedings, was sharply repre-
hended by the Adjutant - General, Brigadier-
General Clinton, for neglect of duty, and accused
of giving false intelligence, as the General insisted that the picquet had been skirmishing with
a body of Spanish cavalry belonging to Romana's
army.*   Whatever the true state of this affair

* Captain Cochrane felt the remarks made by General
Clinton upon his conduct, when commanding the picquet near
Bembibere on January 2, to be so injurious to his character
as an officer, that he applied to the General through Colonel
Grant, in the hope of prevailing upon him to retract the
offensive expressions, and to acknowledge that the censure
was unmerited and had arisen from misconception.   General
Clinton, however, persisted in his former opinion, and repeated
his conviction that Captain Cochrane had behaved in a manner
unbecoming an officer.   The latter in consequence demanded
a court-martial on our return to England, and was tried at
Chelsea in the summer of 1809 on charges preferred against
him by General Clinton.

Captain Cochrane was honourably acquitted by the sentence
of the court, but circumstances have since transpired which
are conclusive in establishing the fact that the troops from
whom Captain Cochrane's picquet retreated were really Spanish
light cavalry, whose uniform bears a strong resemblance to
that of the French *chasseurs à cheval*, and that officer's conduct
was certainly extremely blameable in retiring before he had
fully ascertained that the force in his front was an enemy.
It was said in his defence that the skirmishers of the two
bodies fired upon each other; but this statement, if correct,

may be, it is certain that the chief officers of the staff had adopted an opinion, which amounted to conviction, that the enemy would give over the pursuit as soon as our army entered the defiles of the hilly country beyond Astorga. Any information, therefore, that militated against this favourite tenet was most ungraciously received. The events of this day must have convinced them of their error, although they persisted in maintaining that we were only followed by a few squadrons of Napoleon's cavalry.

Our regiment still formed the rear-guard, and during the march we had a great deal of trouble with the stragglers, numbers of whom were so drunk that all our efforts to drive them on were fruitless, and we were obliged to abandon them to their fate. They were soon overtaken by the French *chasseurs*, who treated them most unmercifully, cutting to their right and left, and sparing none who came within reach of their swords. They were even accused of wounding the sick men whom they overtook in the hospital waggons.

proves the negligent manner in which the reconnaissance was conducted, for if the Spanish patrols had been properly challenged they could not have been mistaken for Frenchmen.

Thomas Smith, an old soldier of my troop, was amongst the number of those left at Bembibere, being too drunk to march with the baggage and dismounted men. He was one of the few Villars-en-Couché men still remaining in the regiment, and did good service at Sahagun, where I saw his sword covered with blood from hilt to point. The plunder he obtained from the men he killed amounted to thirty or forty doubloons, and from that day he was scarcely ever sober. As he was in general a good soldier, I was much vexed at losing him.*

We had some skirmishing with the enemy's advanced guard in the early part of the day, but in the afternoon they pressed us so hard that the regiment was halted, and formed in column of divisions on a small eminence, masking the guns of the horse brigade which were brought up to support us. On observing our position, the enemy retired, and we were ordered to occupy

* However, he contrived to escape from the French, and joined one of the bands of Spaniards who kept up a desultory warfare after the British army quitted the country. Having been wounded in one of these skirmishes, he was at length received on board one of our cruisers, and we were surprised by his appearance at Guildford Barracks about the end of October.

Cubilos, a small village at no great distance, where we found a company of the Ninety-fifth. So many horses had been sent forward, having become unserviceable for want of shoes, that the regiment at this period could scarcely muster four hundred in the field, many of which were lame or quite worn out with fatigue, and the remainder unable to trot. Considering the jaded state of our horses, and the fact that almost the whole of the outpost duty ever since the commencement of the retreat had fallen upon the Fifteenth, it might reasonably have been expected that one of the other regiments should have been appointed to this service; but it seemed to be a settled system of our leaders to save the Tenth and Seventh as much as possible, out of compliment to the Prince of Wales and Lord Paget.

It was almost dark when we arrived at Cubilos, and whilst the quartermasters were making arrangements for getting the troops under cover, the regiment was drawn up in close column on an open space of ground in the centre of the place. We had not remained long in this position, when we were surprised by a quick and irregular discharge of small arms; the bullets rattled against the walls and lodged in the roofs of the houses behind which we were sheltered.

This unexpected attack created a considerable degree of uneasiness, for the horses were so wedged together it was with difficulty they could break into file ; and the communication betwixt the village and the highroad was through a narrow hollow-way, where, if a single horse had fallen, it would have occasioned a scene of confusion which must have led to the most disastrous consequences. Having been ordered for duty, I was engaged in telling off the picquet at a little distance from the column when the firing commenced ; and strong patrols being immediately despatched to the assistance of the riflemen, who were skirmishing with our visitors, the intruders were soon put to flight. After the regiment was withdrawn from the village, it was determined by the commanding officer to bivouac ; it is only extraordinary that under the circumstances he should for a moment have entertained the intention of passing the night in quarters. Three squadrons took up a position near Cubilos ; the left squadron was detached half a mile to the rear, where a road struck off to Ponteferrado. Our advanced picquets and

patrols were pushed close to the French outposts, and shots were exchanged occasionally
when either party encroached too much on the
other's ground. The weather was cold and
frosty, but we collected fuel enough to supply
several large fires; and, as the inhabitants had
deserted their dwellings, we were forced to
plunder the village in order to procure provisions and forage. But this was a necessary
measure, and executed without any breach of
discipline. Working parties were sent under
the orderly officer and quartermasters to break
open the houses, and abundant supplies of bread,
meat, wine, corn, and hay, were found, which
proved highly acceptable both to men and horses,
who had been but scantily provided with sub-
sistence since we left San Christoval.

Of course great havoc was committed on the
property of these poor villagers, for much of
what we could not consume was destroyed, to
prevent our pursuers from having the benefit
of it.

In the middle of the night we were alarmed
by the cracking of whips, the noise of wheels,
and the plashing of horses and carriages in the
River Sil, which flowed at some distance below

Cubilos, on our right. We at first imagined that
the enemy's artillery and infantry had arrived,
and were endeavouring to get in our rear ; but
upon sending out a patrol to ascertain the facts,
the disturbance proved to be caused by part of
Romana's baggage and cannon. One of the
mule-drivers, who was brought to Colonel Grant,
afforded us a great deal of amusement. Believing
that he had fallen into the hands of the French,
he exhibited signs of the greatest terror. He fell
on his knees, wept, and implored our mercy for
the sake of his wife and three infants ; then
kissed the earth, and shouted, " Viva el Señor
Napoleon !" When we had sufficiently diverted
ourselves with his apprehensions, he was set at
liberty without having his mistake rectified.

The next scene we witnessed called forth very
different sensations. A poor wretch was conducted to the officers' fire by a patrol who per-
ceived a figure, which he at first took for a wild
hog, creeping amongst some stunted copse-wood
that bordered the road near our advanced post.
He turned out to be one of the numerous band
of stragglers who had been overtaken and sabred
by the French. He had drawn his shirt over his
head to keep the frosty air from his wounds, and

when the covering was removed from his face, it presented the most shocking spectacle I ever beheld. It was impossible to distinguish a single feature. The flesh of his cheeks and lips was hanging in collops; his nose was slit, and his ears, I think, were cut off. Besides the wounds on his head, he had received many in different parts of the body, and it is surprising that he should have been able to make his escape in the feeble state to which he was reduced by loss of blood.

The unfortunate man was unable to swallow solid food, but we gave him some warm wine, and when he was a little revived by the heat of the fire he was sent to the hospital at Villafranca; but I imagine he had little chance of recovering. In addition to his wounds, it is probable that his limbs were frost-bitten; for it was quite horrible to see the manner in which he cowered near the fire, and raked the glowing embers towards him with his fingers. It was with difficulty he could make himself understood, but we learnt from him that the loiterers had been most barbarously treated by the enemy.

3rd.—Betwixt nine and ten o'clock in the morning we observed the French, formed in three lines, on a rising ground about a mile from the spot we occupied. Our advanced picquet and riflemen had frequent skirmishes with them, but we only wounded three or four men, and they killed one of our horses at the distance of nearly 500 yards, although they had often fired at us within a quarter of the distance and failed. Their guns were longer in the barrel than the firelocks used by our infantry, and appeared to be very good pieces.

An officer of the *chasseurs*, mounted on a fine grey charger, made himself conspicuous by riding along the front to encourage his men, and occasionally galloping forward, as if for the purpose of inviting one of us to meet him in single combat. In our situation it was not judged expedient to allow any officer to answer this challenge; but the sharpshooters endeavoured to pick him off, and at length succeeded in killing his horse, which probably moderated the ardour of the rider, for we saw no more of him. About noon a *fourrier* of the 22nd Chasseurs, who had been wounded in the thigh by a rifle-ball, was brought into our lines. We learned from him that the force opposed to us was a division of cavalry, commanded by General

21

Colbert, and that Marshal Soult was hourly expected to come up with two divisions of infantry. He entreated us to use him well, adding that his countrymen showed the greatest kindness to our people who fell into their hands. Little did he imagine what a specimen we had seen of their tenderness to our stragglers.

As the morning was nearly spent without any communication from headquarters, an officer was despatched to make a report of the hazardous situation in which we were placed, and to bring back orders how we were to act in the case of being attacked ; and whilst we were in expectation of his return General Slade visited the position. I was conversing with Colonel Grant at the time, and in a few minutes Captain Thackwell joined us, with the intelligence that the French were in motion, and that twenty squadrons could be distinctly counted in their lines. Colonel Grant upon this invited the General to ride forward with us and reconnoitre them, which he declined, saying he must go and report the circumstance to the Commander of the Forces. He then clapped spurs to his horse, and was quickly out of sight. We learned that he did not slacken his pace until he met Sir John

Moore, to whom he repeated what he had heard, saying that he was desired by Colonel Grant to report it. Sir John Moore asked the Brigadier how long he had been Colonel Grant's aide-de-camp, and told him that the proper post of a general officer was at the head of his brigade or division when in presence of the enemy. The General, however, considered the Tenth as the head of his brigade, for we saw no more of him.

The French continued to threaten us by various manœuvres until near two o'clock, when orders were received for the regiment to fall back and join the main body of the army at Villafranca. We retired very slowly, to allow the Reserve time to break up their encampment, and the enemy followed at the same pace along the highroad, with a band of music playing at the head of their column. Our rear-guard kept them at bay until, on approaching Cacabelos, the leading squadrons gained a rise in the road, which enabled them to discover the mere handful of troops opposed to them ; upon which they immediately charged, and drove us a few hundred yards, but at the entrance of the town we fronted them, and fought hand to hand, disputing every

inch of ground. For some minutes we were so
jammed together in a narrow street that it was
impossible for either party to advance or retire.
At this period of the conflict one of our men
decapitated a French *chasseur* at a single blow;
the head was not entirely separated, but remained
attached by a muscle or part of the skin of the
neck. General Colbert was also killed by a
carbine or rifle shot. Sir John Moore, Sir David
Baird, Lord Paget, and a number of Generals
and staff officers, were in the plaza when the
Fifteenth entered the town, and only owed their
safety to the determined bravery of the rear-
guard, which checked the advance of the enemy,
and thus afforded time for them to quit the
place. General Paget's troops were cooking
when they received the order to turn out, and,
notwithstanding we retired at a slow walk, to
allow them as much time as possible, we reached
Cacabelos before they had completely taken up
their position. The Ninety-fifth should have
lined a wood on the right of the road leading
to Bembibere, but they were not posted when
the enemy came up, and the *chasseurs* dashed in
upon them and threw them into confusion. Many
of the riflemen, on their discomfiture, instead of

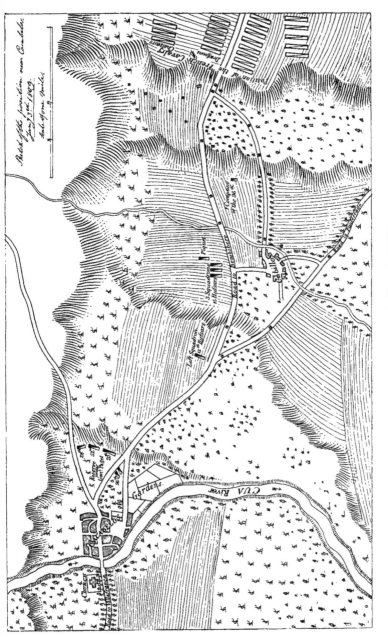

PLAN OF THE ACTION AT CACABELOS.

saving themselves by passing through the gardens and enclosures, ran into the streets, where a number of them were sabred and trampled down by the horses.

As soon as the streets were cleared we crossed the river; two guns of the horse brigade were planted on a height which commanded the bridge, and opened on the French when they attempted to follow us. After sustaining some loss they retired into the town. On this, as well as on many other occasions, we were certainly much indebted to the forbearance of the enemy; for if they had attacked us with spirit, it would have been scarcely possible for the regiment to have escaped annihilation.

We passed through Villafranca without halting; the infantry had evacuated the place, and were in position on the neighbouring heights, which appeared to be impregnable. The town presented the most dreadful scenes of riot and distress. Parties of drunken soldiers were committing all kinds of enormities; several houses were in flames; and a quantity of baggage and military stores, for which there was no means of conveyance, were burning in the plaza. The kennels were flowing with rum, a number of

22

puncheons having been staved in the streets, and a promiscuous rabble were drinking and filling bottles and canteens from the stream. Every avenue was crowded with bât-horses, mules, and bullock-cars.

We now confidently anticipated a respite, for some days at least, from the harassing outpost duty, by which both our men and horses were almost worn out, as it was reckoned a matter of course that the infantry would form the rear-guard through the mountains. We here entered the province of Galicia, and the road for a distance of sixteen leagues presents a constant succession of defiles and strong passes—a description of country by no means adapted for cavalry to act in with advantage. We arrived at Las Herrerias at eight o'clock ; this place is two leagues from Villafranca, and takes its name from the iron-foundries established in the vicinity. We congratulated ourselves on the prospect of passing the night undisturbed, but at ten o'clock the " rouse " was sounded, and we learned, with surprise and indignation, that the whole army, except the 20th and 95th Regiments, had passed through the village in full retreat.

I had suffered all day from rheumatism in the

head; my feet and legs were slightly frost-bitten, and so much swelled that I was forced to have my boots cut open as soon as I got into quarters. Being greatly in need of repose, I went to bed as soon as possible, but had not laid down five minutes before the bugles sounded. My first impulse was to lie still and be taken by the French, rather than encounter a renewal of the fatigues and anxiety we had so lately undergone. This idea, however, was but momentary; I dressed myself without delay, and hastened to the alarm-post.

It was now apparent, notwithstanding the assurances to the contrary with which we had been amused, that there was no intention of making a stand anywhere, but that the only object of our leaders was to gain the coast, and embark the army with as little delay as possible. Surmises of this nature had existed amongst the troops for some days, but the confirmation these suspicions received from the events of the last few hours destroyed the small portion of discipline that still remained, and left them soldiers but in name.

Sir John Moore's conduct in not defending the heights near Villafranca appears to me to admit of no valid excuse; that position might have been maintained for two or three days at least by the Reserve and a proportion of artillery, whilst the cavalry and main body of infantry were retiring by easy marches to Lugo. In this manner time would have been allowed for the men to recover from their fatigue, and opportunities afforded of restoring a sufficient degree of discipline to enable them to continue the retreat with regularity, or to give battle with confidence. Even after quitting Villafranca, every step of the road offered points where a single company of grenadiers, with one or two field-pieces, might have kept an army in check for some hours, and would have given more serious interruption, of course, to a corps of cavalry, unsupported by infantry or artillery. The road for a distance of several leagues wound along the side of steep mountains, and at almost every turn a well-served battery would have caused a heavy loss to an advancing column; and considerable delay might have been occasioned in many places by merely breaking up a few yards of the road. I think it can scarcely admit of a doubt that, if either of these plans had been acted upon, the retreat would have been effected with inconsiderable loss in comparison with that which was actually sustained.

But Sir John Moore, although an officer of eminent bravery and of tried ability in subordinate commands, now that he was called upon to conduct a considerable force in circumstances of peculiar difficulty, proved lamentably deficient in those qualities of decision and firmness which he had so often displayed on former occasions, and which alone could have enabled him to extricate the army by some brilliant achievement, from the perilous situation in which it had been placed by his own ill-advised measures and the disasters of our Spanish allies. At this juncture, however, he appeared to labour under a depression of spirits, so different from his usual serene and cheerful disposition as to give a mournful expression to his countenance, indicative of the greatest anxiety of mind; and it seemed either that his judgment was completely clouded, or that he was under the influence of a spell, which forced him to commit the most glaring errors. The strong position at Villafranca was scarcely occupied before it was determined to abandon it, and no obstacle was opposed to the enemy's movements in a long march through a mountainous district, where the nature of the ground afforded unusual facilities for obstructing the advance of an army. It was generally supposed that the Commander of the Forces was induced to hurry towards Corunna by the apprehension that, in case of delay, the division which occupied the province of Leon might advance through the Asturias, cut off his communications with the coast, and place him betwixt two fires. But he ought not to have been ignorant of the fact that—besides being more than double the distance and passing through a barren and difficult country—the road in question is, after leaving Oviedo, merely a mule-track, passable in the summer season, but quite impracticable for the passage of an army with cavalry and artillery, especially in the depth of winter.

A considerable portion of the night was spent in ascending the long hill of Nogales, which was covered with snow. The cold was most intense, and the wind absolutely piercing. The objects which met the view at almost every step were of a description calculated to shock the firmest mind, and had we been differently circumstanced must have excited the most active sympathy;

but the frequent recurrence of scenes of misery, and our own individual privations and sufferings, had so far deadened the kindly feelings of our nature that we witnessed without emotion the wretchedness by which we were surrounded.

We passed a number of cars filled with sick and wounded soldiers stuck fast in the drifted snow ; many of these unfortunate men perished from the severity of the weather. Several of Romana's cannon were left on this mountain, the animals which dragged them having perished or become unserviceable. One of the pieces had been overturned, and an artilleryman was lying under it, crushed to death. Some cars laden with specie, and a great quantity of stores and baggage, were also abandoned to the enemy.

During this distressful night-march I repeatedly observed soldiers, spent with fatigue or insensible from the effects of intoxication, lying on the snow, whence they were fated never to rise ; and the road was often obstructed by the mangled carcasses of horses and mules. The women who followed the army displayed astonishing energy, but the sufferings they endured beggar all description. This night proved fatal to many of these unfortunate creatures. One of them, who had been delivered of twins only three days before, and another with an infant at her breast, were amongst the victims. The children in both instances were alive when discovered, and owed their preservation to the humanity of some infantry soldiers.

During a temporary halt shortly after daybreak, I had some conversation with an officer who commanded a small party stationed near the road ; he told me that his regiment—I do not recollect the number—which had been two days without provisions, was in bivouac on the mountain, and that two officers and a number of privates had perished during the night from the combined effects of cold, hunger, and fatigue.

CHAPTER V

[*From the* 6th *to the* 8th *the army remained halted
at Lugo, where Moore offered battle to Soult, and
the British regiments recovered something of their
discipline and collected many of their stragglers.
The French Marshal hesitated to attack, and, on the
night of the* 8th, *Moore, who had no more than one
day's supplies in Lugo, resumed the retreat. The
army reached Betanzos on the* 9th, *and on the night
of the* 11th *the main body marched into Corunna,
where the transports had not yet arrived from Vigo.
The fleet of transports came in on the* 14th, *and the
work of embarkation was commenced as early as
practicable. On this day the French appeared before
the town, attacked our advanced positions on the* 15th,
*and delivered battle on the day following—a battle
which was so far successful that it secured for the
British an unmolested embarkation, but which cost
the life of Sir John Moore, and which, though its
success redeemed the honour of the British arms,
could not altogether atone for the failure of the
expedition and the humiliations and disgrace of the
retreat.*]

January 4th.—We entered Las Nogales about nine o'clock, and, after halting there for two hours to feed the horses, continued our route to Constantino, where we arrived betwixt three and four, having marched sixty-four miles in twenty-five hours, twenty-two of which we were actually on horseback. Taking all the circumstances into consideration, this may be looked upon as an extraordinary performance both for men and horses, particularly as the pace never exceeded a walk. The Fifteenth halted at Constantino, but the remainder of the cavalry and the infantry proceeded to Lugo. An unsuccessful attempt was made to blow up the fine bridge betwixt Nogales and Constantino, and the failure in this instance cannot be a subject of regret, as it would have been a thousand pities to have destroyed so beautiful an object, particularly as the progress of the enemy could not have been materially checked by its demolition.

Near this spot the guns of the mule brigade, as it was called, which had never been fired, were spiked and thrown down a precipice. These pieces, three-pounders, were remarkably light, and constructed so as to be conveyed on the backs of mules, through roads and into positions inaccessible to ordinary artillery. Three mules were attached to each gun; one carried the barrel, another the carriage, and the third was loaded with ammunition. Several casks of dollars and doubloons were also rolled down the steep side of the road into the valley beneath, just in time to prevent their capture.

Lord Paget and Brigadier-General Stewart, both disabled by ophthalmia, which was very prevalent amongst the troops, passed us on the march. The former looked very interesting; he had a white handkerchief bound over his eyes, and Colonel Elley, the Adjutant-General to the cavalry, led his horse.

A squadron of the Fifteenth was left at Nogales, and, with some companies of the Ninety-fifth, formed the rear-guard of the army from that place. They were directed to retire if pressed, but to seize every opportunity of impeding the enemy's advance, in order to allow as much time as possible for the repose and refreshment of the preceding divisions.

Our quarters at Constantino were wretched in the extreme, and our fare was of the same description; but any kind of food or shelter was acceptable to men worn out with fatigue and

almost starved. It had rained without intermission the greatest part of the day, but at two
o'clock it came down with a degree of violence
that our horses could scarcely face.

I had suffered such agony for many hours
from an attack of rheumatism in the head that
my strength and spirits were entirely exhausted,
and I felt thankful at being able to obtain a
share of some wet straw in the narrow loft of
a miserable hovel, which was occupied by at
least a dozen persons—officers, soldiers, and
servants—all distinction of ranks being levelled
by the distress and danger to which all were
equally exposed.

5th.—The regiment marched from Constantino
at eight o'clock, and reached Lugo at two in the
afternoon. The town was crowded with troops,
and, as every house and stable were occupied by
the divisions which had arrived the night before,
we, who had performed almost the whole of the
duty allotted to the cavalry in covering the
retreat since the army marched from Astorga,
found it impossible to procure quarters, either
for men or horses. We were therefore obliged
to be contented with the shelter afforded by the
piazzas in the plaza during our halt at this p lace.

All the straggling and irregularities that had occurred on any former occasion might be considered as the perfection of discipline if compared with the retreat from Villafranca, which resembled the flight of an indisciplined rabble rather than the march of regular troops; and a comparison drawn at this period betwixt the British army and Romana's mob would not have been much in favour of the former. The loss on this single march probably fell but little short of 2,000 men. This increased disorganization may be in part accounted for by the indignation of the troops at what they considered a breach of faith on the part of the Commander of the Forces, who had given repeated assurances that he had no intention of withdrawing the army from Spain, but that his object in retreating was to approach his supplies, and take up a position which should enable him to oppose the superior numbers brought against him, with a reasonable prospect of success. When, however, they saw the most favourable ground for defensive operations abandoned without even a show of resistance, the men lost all confidence in a General who neglected to seize and improve opportunities which every private soldier was

23

capable of appreciating. The general orders issued during the retreat sufficiently mark Sir John Moore's sense of the insubordination of the troops; but I must consider his own vacillating conduct as the primary cause of the evil, which was increased by a culpable lenity towards flagrant offenders, the effect of which was to encourage breaches of discipline. At length, when the army was considerably reduced in numbers, broken in spirit, and weakened in physical power by excessive fatigue and the want of provisions, it was determined to make a stand at Lugo; the Commander of the Forces being now convinced that, in the exhausted condition of the men and horses, it was impossible to continue the retreat without exposing his whole force to certain destruction. General Fraser's division, which had proceeded a day's march on the road to Vigo, was therefore recalled, and the whole of the baggage was sent forward to Corunna, with the sick and all those who were unfit for duty.

One of the most absurd orders that ever was issued in our service—and that is saying a great deal—directed all dismounted dragoons to join the Ninety-fifth and act as sharpshooters !

6th.—The rear-guard, which had been repeatedly engaged with the head of the French column since they left Nogales, joined us about ten o'clock, and the enemy made their appearance in the afternoon, but nothing of importance occurred.

This day was employed in reorganizing the several corps, and replacing the various articles of equipment which had been lost or become unserviceable during the retreat. Many of the inhabitants had deserted their houses, and those who remained did not appear to bear us much good-will. Most of the shops were shut up, and business of all kind was at a standstill; provisions were scarce, but the troops received biscuit, rum, and salt beef, from the sea-stores, which had been ordered to meet us here. A great number of horses and mules that were lame, or in other respects unfit for service, were shot, and the streets and roads near the city were much obstructed by their carcasses.

The general orders reflected most severely on the conduct of regimental officers, to whose inattention and neglect of their duties the Commander of the Forces chiefly attributed the irregularities of the troops. This censure, which

gave great offence to a considerable portion of
the army, was equally ill-judged and unjust.
The officers of every rank exerted themselves to
the utmost of their ability to preserve order and
secure the comfort of the soldiers ; but when all
the circumstances of our situation are taken into
consideration—the length and rapidity of the
marches, the want of rest and scanty supply
of provisions, the severity of the weather and
dreadful state of the roads—it must be allowed
that it was not possible for the officers, who
encountered the same hardships and privations,
to superintend the conduct of their men in the
manner they are accustomed to do in barracks
or quarters in England.

7th.—A strong corps of the French army,
having arrived in the night, took up a position
on the hills near Lugo, and about eleven o'clock
commenced a cannonade, which was soon silenced
by our artillery. In the afternoon they made a
vigorous attack on our position, but were repulsed
with considerable loss. The cavalry was ordered
out, and the Fifteenth was posted on a rising
ground separated from the enemy by a narrow
valley. As we marched along the front of the
line to gain our station, we passed Sir John

Moore and his staff engaged in reconnoitring; they were accompanied by a lady mounted on a white charger, who I understood was the wife of Colonel Mackenzie, of the 5th Regiment. She betrayed no signs of uneasiness, although the enemy sent a few balls at the party.

Whilst we were on the march to our station in the line, I felt an unusual depression of spirits, which it was quite out of my power to overcome. This despondency of mind was probably occasioned by fatigue and bodily suffering, but it produced such strong conviction of impending evil that I desired Baron During to remain near me, and entreated him, in case I should fall, not to suffer me to be left on the field disabled. These melancholy forebodings, however, proved groundless; not even a skirmish took place, and we returned to our quarters early in the evening.

8th.—At six o'clock the cavalry assembled, and marched from Lugo to take up the same position we had occupied the evening before; and although the pain in my head was even more excruciating, I experienced none of those gloomy presages.

A great portion of the infantry had bivouacked on the ground, and in proceeding to our station

24

we passed along the front of the line, which afforded us an opportunity of observing the disposition of the men. Nothing could be more gratifying than to remark the total change in their conduct. It appeared that, with the prospect of being led against the foe, they had at once recovered all those qualities for which British soldiers are peculiarly estimable; every order was obeyed with alacrity, and not a trace remained of the discontent and insubordination which had been so general for the past few days. Both officers and men expressed the most ardent desire to bring the contest to an issue, and, notwithstanding the inferiority of our numbers, a confident anticipation of victory filled every breast. The French, however, did not think fit to accept the battle we offered, but remained under arms in their position, which was too strong to be attacked without great loss. Besides, Marshal Soult had it in his power to decline a general action, even if we had succeeded in carrying the heights; and it is most probable he would have fallen back, and endeavoured to amuse us until the arrival of the divisions in his rear, which would have placed him at the head of an overwhelming force. His best policy was, undoubtedly, to avoid fighting, since by continuing to harass our retreat he might expect to reap all the advantages of a decisive victory without the hazard of a battle.

We passed the day in a state of anxious suspense, impatiently listening for the roar of artillery, which we expected to mark the commencement of the action; and, as hour after hour elapsed without any demonstration on either side, a universal feeling of the most bitter disappointment spread through the ranks.

The Fifteenth did not muster above 200 men, and was posted on the extreme left of the line, nearly two miles distant from any support; our horses were quite knocked up, and we probably had cause to be thankful that we were not attacked by a strong body of the enemy's cavalry to which we were opposed, although we did not think so at the time.

In the course of the day the men's valises and haversacks were searched, but, highly to the credit of the regiment, not a single article of plunder was discovered.

Sir John Moore, finding that he could not entice Marshal Soult from his vantage-ground, and not judging it advisable to attack his position, had no other alternative but to continue the retreat, as the provisions which had been collected at Lugo were nearly exhausted, and we could only obtain supplies from Corunna.

Orders were accordingly given to withdraw the guns as soon as the evening closed in sufficiently to mask the movement, and the troops began their march about nine o'clock. Watch-fires were left burning on the ground we had occupied, which were kept up during the night by the picquets, who remained to observe the enemy's motions. The different columns retired with the utmost regularity, and in such perfect silence that the French did not discover our evasion until after daylight. The night was extremely dark, which favoured this manœuvre. Our route to the town lay over broken ground and through intricate lanes; the country was also much intersected by dry stone walls, enclosing the fields and vineyards, which made it difficult to keep the squadrons together, as no man could see his own horse's head, much less his file leader.

Our regiment was destined to form the rear-guard as usual, and halted under the walls of Lugo, near the Corunna Gate, at eleven o'clock, to allow time for the infantry, who had not yet come up, to join the line of march. During this interval the left squadron was ordered to the town-house to take charge of 35,000 dollars, which must otherwise have been left as a prize for the enemy. Sealed bags, each containing 500 dollars, were distributed to the troopers, and in this manner about £8,000 was saved to the nation; but our poor horses were much oppressed by the addition of nearly two stone to the weight they already carried.

9th.—Some of the columns lost their way, owing to the darkness of the night and the mistakes of the guides, so that it was near two o'clock before they all got clear of the town. We followed soon afterwards, and on crossing the Mino found the Engineers employed in mining the bridge. It was natural to suppose that, after so many failures, they had acquired sufficient experience to enable them to accomplish their object, and in this instance success was particularly desirable, as the river was not fordable. The stream is broad and rapid, the bank rotten, and the neighbourhood does not furnish material for making even a temporary repair. The destruction of this bridge was there fore expected to throw considerable impediments in the way of the enemy's advance; but our hopes were again disappointed. The powder exploded, the bridge remained uninjured, and the French crossed the river within a few hours after us. It is an extraordinary circumstance that our Engineers, who bear such a high character, should have failed so frequently in one of the most simple operations of the science.*

Colonel Dud'huit, of the 8th Dragoons, was at Lugo when we arrived there, and, being unwell, obtained permission to remain with the army on his parole, instead of accompanying the escort with the rest of the prisoners to Corunna. Major Leitch, who had been the means of procuring him this indulgence, considering himself in some measure responsible for the captive's fidelity, went to his quarters to see if he was preparing to follow us, and found him in bed. The Colonel complained of indisposition, and endeavoured to prevail upon Leitch to consent to his remaining at Lugo, promising solemnly

* The failures here adverted to are stated to have been caused by the deficiency of the necessary implements and the want of sappers.

not to give his countrymen the slightest information relative to the state of our army.
Such a proposal could not be acceded to, and the
Major was obliged to insist upon his joining our
column ; but, as he was not confined to any particular station in the line of march, he might
have quitted the road and concealed himself,
until he had an opportunity of escaping to the
French cavalry who led the pursuit.   Either his
sense of honour was too strong to allow him to
break his parole, or he was deterred by the
fear of being discovered and murdered by the
Spaniards, of whose resentment he always expressed the liveliest apprehensions.

Whilst the regiment was waiting under the
walls of Lugo, Baron During rode into the town
to endeavour to procure some bread, and, as he
did not return before we moved, I began to fear
he had been intercepted by a French patrol, or
that some other misfortune had happened to
him ; but, to my great satisfaction, he rejoined us
on the march, although in a very unsavoury
condition, owing to a fall over some dead horses
in the streets of Lugo.

This night-march was productive of a repe-
tition of the hardships we had before experienced,

and the straggling and disorderly conduct of the troops was carried to an alarming extent. We passed through Bamonde without stopping, and reached Gutoriez at one o'clock in the afternoon, in the midst of the most violent storm of hail and rain I ever witnessed.

About 200 of our horses found shelter in a large stable at the posada ; the house was crowded with officers and soldiers. Sir David Baird and his staff occupied all the apartments, so that we were obliged to be contented with the accommodation afforded by the kitchen and passages. I had been so fortunate as to obtain a place near the fire, round which a number of officers and men of different corps were assembled to dry their clothes and thaw their half-frozen limbs ; but we were soon disturbed by Sir David Baird's cook, who insisted upon having the fire entirely to herself, that she might boil his tea-kettle. She was so violently enraged at our non - compliance with this unreasonable demand that, after scolding herself out of breath, she retired in great dudgeon.

In a few minutes an aide-de-camp appeared, who informed us that Sir David Baird desired we would all quit the house, which had been

allotted for his quarters. However excusable
such a stretch of authority might have been in
ordinary circumstances, we felt that in our situation it was carrying the privileges of military
rank too far, and no one seemed inclined to
exchange the comparative comfort of the place
we occupied for a bivouac in the open street,
exposed to the pelting of the storm, merely to
gratify the spleen of Sir David's cook. Brigadier-
General Fane, who was one of the party, remon-
strated with the aide-de-camp* on the harshness
and indelicacy of sending such a message to a
number of officers, and *he*, who seemed uncomfortable at being obliged to deliver it, quitted
the room without insisting on our departure.

At eleven o'clock the bugles sounded, when
the cavalry turned out, and remained mounted
whilst the infantry filed past us, which was a
very tedious business. Several men perished
from the effects of intoxication and the severity
of the weather during the few hours the army
occupied the village of Gutoriez and adjacent
fields; two private hussars of the Fifteenth were
amongst the number.

* The aide-de-camp was Captain Hon. Alexander Gordon,
3rd Guards (afterwards mortally wounded at Waterloo).—Ed.

10*th.*—After another dreadful night-march, we reached Betanzos about three o'clock p.m., having been nearly sixteen hours in accomplishing a distance of five leagues. The miseries to which the troops were exposed increased at every step. The road, which had excited my admiration a few weeks before, was now so completely broken up by the frequent changes of the weather from frost to thaw, and the continual passing of heavy carriages, that the soldiers were often obliged to wade through mud more than a foot in depth. Many of the officers were destitute of shoes or stockings, with their clothes in rags ; it may therefore be imagined that the privates were in a most deplorable condition. Straggling had increased to such a degree that, if the retreat had continued three days longer, the army must have been totally annihilated. The men were so much exhausted by incessant fatigue and want of food, added to the effects of a violent dysentery which raged amongst them, that many who lay down to rest themselves at a little distance from the roadside had not sufficient strength to rejoin the line of march, and fell into the hands of the enemy. Soldiers of different corps were mixed promiscuously together, and the Colours of one

regiment—the Fiftieth, I think—entered Betanzos without a single man to form to them.
Contrary to my expectations, the men of the
Highland Brigade lagged as much as those of
other regiments.

The Guards bore up against all these hardships
far better than the rest of the army. Their
ranks were always well closed, and the battalions
mustered strong ; they lost comparatively few of
their number by straggling. The same may be
said of the Light Brigade and of all the regiments
which formed the Reserve.

The Engineers at length succeeded in blowing
up a bridge near Betanzos ; but this success cost
more than it was worth, since an officer and two
or three men were killed by the explosion, and
a picquet of our regiment which came up soon
afterwards forded the stream without difficulty.

The ignorance displayed by the general staff
with respect to the resources of the country and
the state of the roads and rivers, etc., was quite
inexcusable, and was one of the chief causes of
the miseries suffered by the army during the
retreat. The incapacity of this branch of our
service and of our commissariat appeared more
manifestly from the different manner in which

the duties of these departments are conducted in
the French army.

On approaching Betanzos we found several
regiments of infantry *en bivouac ;* the remainder
of the army occupied the town and filled almost
every house.   We had therefore great difficulty in
getting quarters for our men and horses, and when
that object was accomplished, Baron During and
myself, after many unsuccessful trials, began to
despair of finding accommodation for ourselves,
when, happening to meet Captain Dalrymple, he
proposed to us to accompany him to a house
where he had been billeted when the regiment
halted in the place on the advance of the army.
As this house stood in the outskirts of the town,
there was some chance that it might still remain
unoccupied.   We therefore hastened thither, and
only found a few non-commissioned officers
and privates of the 10th and 18th Hussars,
who were established in the lower apartments.
Having ascertained that there was good stabling
for our horses, we made our way upstairs to a
room where five or six ecclesiastics were sitting
round a table, covered with the fragments of a
very substantial repast ; our appetites were too
keen to allow us to stand upon ceremony, and

we scarcely waited for an invitation to join the party.

Our hosts displayed extreme uneasiness at the rapid approach of the enemy, and soon took leave of us to prepare for their departure to Ferrol. The greater part of the furniture had been already removed, so that in most of the apartments nothing was to be seen except the bare walls. I soon discovered that we were in the very house where I had passed the evening at a *tertulla* on November 23, the day on which I left Corunna, with expectations and feelings very different from those I now entertained.

Although I suffered severely from rheumatism in the head, and was still very lame from my legs having been frost-bitten, my spirits never flagged, except when I was almost distracted by the violence of the pain; nay, so unaccountable is the economy of the human mind, that I may say I never felt more free from care and anxiety than during this retreat, when exposed to hardships and privations of every sort, and sensible that each hour was likely to produce some additional evil.

Notwithstanding the need we had of repose after the fatigues of the three preceding days,

25

we were so much disturbed by repeated false alarms that I obtained very little rest, and was glad when the sound of the bugles summoned us to horse.

11*th*.—The troops assembled for the march before daylight, and reached Corunna about two o'clock p.m. Our poor Brigadier looked very disconsolate, in consequence, as I understood, of the harsh and unjustifiable manner in which he had been treated by Lord Paget under the following circumstances : on our arrival at Betanzos, General Slade, on the plea of indisposition, obtained leave from Sir John Moore to proceed to Corunna, and having established himself in comfortable quarters, took a dose of calomel, and retired to bed. When Lord Paget —who had quitted the army some days before in consequence of an attack of ophthalmia—was informed of the General's arrival, he sent him a peremptory order to return to his brigade without a moment's delay ; and forced him to set out at night, in a soaking rain, regardless of his pathetic remonstrances and intestinal commotions !

The bridge over the Burgo, a small river about two leagues from Betanzos, was blown up after the army crossed it; by this obstacle the enemy's progress was delayed for several hours, which afforded a very seasonable respite to our harassed soldiers. In the early part of the day the French *chasseurs* came so near the rear of our column, that Sir David Baird's travelling carriage and baggage, which had fallen a little behind, were taken by them.

New vigour appeared to be suddenly infused into our ranks, and a lengthened shout of exultation burst from the troops when, upon reaching the summit of a hill about a league from Corunna, we descried that element upon which the British flag reigns unrivalled, and distinguished its colours on the vessels in the bay. But our joy was soon damped, for on approaching the harbour we found there only twenty or thirty sail of transports; and we had the mortification of hearing from naval officers that there was little probability of the fleet we expected arriving for several days, as the voyage from Vigo to Corunna often proves tedious.

The Fifteenth embarked five hundred and sixty troop horses at Portsmouth, and up to this period we had not lost above one hundred; but as more than half the remainder were considered unfit for service, chiefly from want of shoes, we scarcely mustered two hundred mounted in the field.   Lieutenant-Colonel Grant, Major Leitch, Captains Dalrymple and Gordon, Lieutenants Hancox, During, L. P. Jones, and Carpenter, were the only officers who did duty throughout the campaign, and marched into Corunna with the Regiment.

The same spirit of patriotism and hatred towards the invaders still predominated in the breasts of the inhabitants, who were actively employed in putting the fortifications into the best state of defence that time and circumstances would admit.   They expressed a fixed determination to be buried under the ruins of their ramparts rather than submit to the enemy.

12th.—The first division of the French army showed itself in the morning on the right bank of the Burgo, in consequence of which the greatest part of the infantry was ordered out of the town, and took up a position on some hills, about two miles in advance, in order to cover the place.   The enemy's force was hourly augmenting, and frequent skirmishes took place at the outposts, but nothing of importance occurred. In the meantime we were anxiously expecting the arrival of the fleet from Vigo, as our situation became more critical every day, cooped up as we were in a narrow nook of land, nearly surrounded by the ocean, and pressed by a superior force, which we could not attack except at a manifest disadvantage. Provisions of all kinds were extremely scarce, and the small district from which our supplies were drawn was completely exhausted. Bread could hardly be obtained at any price, and fuel began to fail, so that we had the agreeable prospect of starving from the effects both of cold and hunger.

13th.—The whole town was thrown into considerable alarm about nine o'clock this morning by a tremendous explosion, which shook the buildings like an earthquake ; a number of windows were broken by the concussion, and the inhabitants of both sexes rushed into the streets—many of them only half-dressed and with terror in their countenances—and falling on their knees, began to repeat their "Aves" with an energy proportioned to their fright. I was at breakfast at the time this happened, and the idea which first suggested itself to my mind was that the enemy was bombarding the town, and that a shell had fallen upon the house ;

26

but as the crash was not repeated, I attributed it to the real cause, and on reaching a point which commanded a view of the country towards our lines, an immense column of black smoke, which marked the site of the explosion, was slowly rolling away. As the sky was bright and the air quite calm, the cloud it formed rose to an immense height, and did not disperse for a considerable time.

The account I heard of the cause of this explosion, which had thrown all Corunna into a state of alarm, was that Sir John Moore had ordered a magazine to be destroyed which stood in advance of our position, as there was not time to remove the powder it contained, amounting to 1,500 barrels. It was said, however, that there was another depot of nearly 5,000 barrels in an adjoining building, but that this circumstance was concealed from our artillery, who were charged with the execution of the order by the Spanish officer who had charge of the magazine. The consequence was that the fire communicated to this immense quantity of powder, which caused an explosion infinitely more violent in its effects than had been calculated. Some of the men who were employed on this occasion were blown up. The inhabitants of the village in which the magazines were situated had been sufficiently warned of their danger, and desired to remove ; but they paid little attention to the cautions they received, and it is probable many of them perished owing to their obstinacy, as the place was reduced to a heap of ruins.

14th.—The enemy, having repaired the bridge, crossed the Burgo, and took up a strong position on a range of hills which commanded the heights occupied by our army. The fleet which had been so anxiously expected entered the harbour in the afternoon, and the embarkation of the sick commenced immediately ; part of the guns and horses were also got on board before night. A pretty sharp affair of posts took place, in which the French suffered severely.

15th.—The remainder of the artillery and cavalry were embarked. The horse artillery and waggon-train shipped all their horses which were worth bringing away. The officers of the cavalry were allowed to take all their horses, but the number of troop-horses was limited. The Seventh and Tenth embarked ninety, the Fifteenth thirty, the Eighteenth and Third Germans not one. Many hundred fine animals were shot

to prevent the French from benefiting by their
services; and in executing the order for the
destruction of these irrational companions of
their toils, the hearts of the soldiers were more
affected with feelings of pity and grief than by
all the calamities and misery they had witnessed
during the retreat. On this occasion the town
exhibited the appearance of a vast slaughter-
house. Wounded horses, mad with pain, were to
be seen running through the streets, and the
ground was covered with mangled carcasses of
these noble animals; for, in consequence of their
uncertain aim with the pistol, the men were
latterly directed to cut the throats of the horses
instead of attempting to shoot them.

In the evening an unsuccessful attack was
directed against the French advanced posts, in
which Colonel Mackenzie, of the 5th Regiment,
was killed, and his loss, I believe, was greatly
lamented.

16th.—My regiment embarked on the 15th,
and peremptory orders were issued directing all
officers to repair on board the transports to join
their respective troops. I wished to remain on
shore until the embarkation of the infantry was
effected, as I was anxious to be on the spot in

case there should be an engagement, although there seemed little probability of such an event ; but I was obliged reluctantly to bid adieu to Corunna early in the afternoon, and to proceed to my floating dungeon, where I was speedily driven below by violent attacks of sea-sickness.

Our expectations of being allowed to leave the country without fighting proved fallacious ; for the enemy, having received considerable reinforcements, advanced in four columns, and Marshal Soult commenced the action about three o'clock p.m. by an attempt to gain the village of Elvina, on which the right of our army rested. Being completely baffled in that quarter by Lord William Bentinck's brigade, the Guards, and the Reserve, he next attacked the centre, where he was also repulsed ; and after making a desperate effort against the left, with no better success, he retreated, leaving the British in possession of the field of battle. The darkness of the night secured the French from pursuit, but their loss was very severe ; and considering their superiority in number and the disadvantages of our position, the action reflected the highest credit on the troops which were engaged. Sir David Baird was wounded at an early period of the engagement. Shortly afterwards Sir John Moore received a mortal wound; but Sir John Hope, who succeeded to the command, was fully equal to the arduous post, and not only brought the action to a glorious termination, but conducted the subsequent embarkation of the army with such ability, that no operation of the same kind was ever performed in the presence of a superior enemy with more complete success. To this, however, the exertions of the navy contributed most essentially.

About ten o'clock the troops began their march to the beach, leaving strong picquets to observe the enemy; and in the course of the night the whole of the wounded who were in a state to be removed were got on board the fleet. All the ships' boats were employed upon this service, and the master of our vessel, on his return, brought us the first account of the engagement. During the night the greatest part of the army was embarked, and before morning on the 18th the rear-guard stepped into the boats without having experienced the slightest molestation from the enemy.

17th.—The French did not show themselves until the morning was pretty well advanced, when, finding that all our posts were called in, they pushed forward some troops and artillery to the heights above St. Lucia, and opened a cannonade upon the shipping in the harbour, which caused great confusion amongst the transports. Many were obliged to cut their cables, some suffered damage by running foul of each other, and five or six were abandoned by their crews and drifted on shore. The whole of this disorder was occasioned by the bad conduct of the masters of the vessels, who paid no attention to the signals to " weigh anchor and stand into the bay," which had been made repeatedly since break of day. Baron During, who had been left with a small cavalry picquet on the extreme right of the position our army had occupied, did not quit his post until after daylight, and had the bad luck to get on board one of the ships within range of shot from the French battery. The master and part of his crew took to their boat as soon as the firing commenced, leaving the soldiers to get out of the scrape as well as they could by their own exertions. It was at length resolved to cut the cable, when the vessel drifted on the rocks under the castle of St. Antonio, where the Baron and his party remained until relieved from their perilous situation by the long-boat of a man-of-war, which placed them in safety on another transport.

Owing to the circumstances under which the embarkation took place, the troops were necessarily much intermixed and unequally distributed amongst the shipping. It was intended to have rectified these irregularities in the offing; but it came on to blow a hard gale, and any alteration of the arrangements was rendered impracticable. It thus happened that some of the transports came home empty, whilst others carried more than double the number of men for which they were intended; those on board were, in consequence, very uncomfortably situated, particularly the sick and wounded, many of whom suffered materially from the crowded state of the ships. Had the voyage been protracted by any unfavourable occurrence, the troops would have been reduced to a short allowance of provisions, in addition to the other hardships they had to encounter. The fleet was so scantily provided with sea-stores, that the vessel in which I came home had not above a week's supply remaining when we arrived at Portsmouth, although she had but a few more than her complement on board.

Captain Murray and myself, with about forty of our hussars, were in the *Martha*, a small brig betwixt seventy and eighty tons burthen. The fleet was ordered to lay to at the mouth of the harbour, but as the gale increased we made sail from the convoy in the night, and anchored in Stokes Bay about three o'clock p.m. on the 24th, after a favourable passage, during which nothing worthy of notice occurred. Only two or three hospital ships had come into port before us; we had, therefore, no superior officer to control us, and as neither Murray nor myself had been able to sit up since we left Corunna, we lost no time in getting on shore, and felt extraordinary delight at finding ourselves once more on British ground.

On the 25th a great number of transports came into the bay. On the 26th there was a violent storm; many of the ships parted their cables, and were stranded on the beach. The swell was so great that a 74-gun ship broke from the mooring-chains in the harbour, and drifted nearly up to the dockyard. The gale continued some days; several of the fleet were wrecked, and others incurred imminent danger. One of our transports was carried through the Race of Portland, and narrowly escaped ship-

wreck. The vessel with the staff of the regiment on board, would have been driven ashore
on the Isle of Wight but for the vigilance of
Paymaster Henslow, who pointed out the light
at the Needles, which the master had mistaken
for a star; nor could he be fully persuaded of
his error until the ship was close upon the rocks
and in great danger. The ignorance of the ship-
masters in general was so gross that it is surprising so few of the vessels were lost, especially
when it is considered that they were ill-manned,
their sails and rigging in the worst state, and
many of them scarcely seaworthy. A transport
with a detachment of the 7th Hussars on board
struck on the Ram-head, near Plymouth; very
few of the crew were saved, and Major Cavendish, Captain Dukenfield, and Lieutenant
Waldegrave were unfortunately drowned. It
was at first intended that the fleet should proceed to the Downs before the troops were
landed; but in consequence of the sickly state
of the men and the boisterous weather, that plan
was abandoned, and they were ordered to dis-
embark at the first port the vessels put in to.
A route was received for the Fifteenth to proceed
to Romford, and the men of the regiment who

were on board the ships already arrived at Portsmouth were landed on the 31st.

On February 1 we commenced the march to reoccupy our old quarters, but in a very different state from that we appeared in when we traversed the same road three months before. *Then*, well mounted, completely equipped, and filled with anticipations of future glory, we moved in all the "pride, pomp, and circumstance of war." *Now — quantum mutati ab illis —* reduced in numbers, weakened by sickness, baffled in our hopes of fame, ragged, and on foot, we bore no resemblance to our former state. Yet the Fifteenth probably suffered as little as, or less than, any corps employed in this ill-fated expedition, and, but for the destruction of our horses, might have been again fit for service in a very short period. In fact, it was proposed to dismount the 11th, 12th, and 13th Light Dragoons, in order that their horses might be given to the Hussar brigade, which was then to have been sent out to join the troops in Portugal ; but the idea was dropped in consequence of the discontent to which it was likely to give rise.

The loss of the army during the retreat appears, from the returns made to the Adjutant-

General's office on our arrival at Corunna, to have exceeded 5,000 men; and General Craufurd's Division, which sailed from Vigo, is said to have lost above 500 betwixt Ponteferrado and their place of embarkation. Our loss on the 16th is stated at 800 in Sir John Hope's official letter; but I imagine it is understated, and that, including those left at Corunna, our actual loss in killed and wounded exceeded 1,000 men. The public will probably never be accurately informed of the number lost by shipwreck and disease; but I was informed by Dr. Plenderleath, a physician to the forces, that at one period of his attendance at Haslar Hospital the average number of deaths was fifteen daily. The loss of baggage, arms, ammunition, specie, and stores of every description was immense, and above 5,000 horses and mules were destroyed or died of fatigue.

I have frequently heard it asserted by the advocates of Sir John Moore that the plan traced out for him was so ill-conceived, and the points of debarkation and of action so injudiciously selected, that success was altogether unattainable, especially after the defeat and dispersion of all the patriot forces. But even if this be admitted, I am fully persuaded that the distresses the army encountered are chiefly to be attributed to the misconduct of its leader. It may appear invidious to reflect upon the character of an amiable and gallant officer, whose death in the moment of victory has cast a veil of glory over the errors of his judgment; but it is only an act of justice towards the brave men he commanded to point out the causes of the misbehaviour which, unhappily, tarnished their fame. The facts that fell under my own observation are amply sufficient to convict the general staff of incapacity or most culpable neglect of their duties; and owing to the ignorance and inactivity of the commissariat department the troops were frequently in want of food, even when supplies might have been procured without difficulty.

So fine and well appointed an army as that under the command of Sir John Moore was probably never sent into the field either by this or any other nation; but in the short space of four weeks—from the day on which the several corps were united—this force, which both for its appearance and behaviour had been the admiration of all who saw it, after a race of 260 miles, without having been engaged and almost without having seen an enemy, embarked with the loss of the greater part of its baggage and stores, nearly a fourth of its numbers, and the remainder enfeebled by famine and disease. Yet this army, at the point of embarkation, in a disadvantageous position, and almost without artillery, defeated the very enemy from whom it had so disgracefully retreated. Such a complete disorganization of a well-disciplined army in so short a space of time, such a lamentable change in the character of the soldiers, can only be ascribed to the ill-judged precipitancy of the retreat, and the undecided measures of the commander, by which he forfeited the confidence of his troops.

If the campaign was but of short duration, the service during the time it lasted was uncommonly severe. The French dragoons who fell into our hands declared that they scarcely suffered more from cold amidst the snows of Poland in 1806-07. Notwithstanding, our troops evinced the greatest gallantry whenever they were allowed an opportunity; and although the Battle of Corunna was gained under circumstances which eminently proved the superiority of the British soldier, still, I fear the result of this expedition will not increase our military reputation on the Continent. The French have such facilities for circulating their own account of the events in Spain, and their ruler is so little scrupulous of misrepresenting facts to serve his own purposes, that we may expect foreigners will receive impressions on the subject very different from the truth. And, unfortunately, the state of the army not only precluded all thought of improving our success, but afforded some ground for the remark in the *Moniteur* on the *London Gazette* account of the action, that " This victory had all the consequences of the most signal defeat."

The attempt on the part of our Government to assist the Spaniards in their efforts to drive the Gallic invader from their soil has occasioned the loss of immense treasure and thousands of valuable lives, without obtaining the slightest advantage for this country in return, or benefiting the cause we intended to serve. We have also the mortification of feeling that the rapidity of our retreat and subsequent embarkation, added to the excesses committed by our troops on many occasions, have drawn upon us the suspicion and dislike of the very people in whose behalf we have sacrificed so much, and whose gratitude at least we were entitled to expect.

APPENDICES

APPENDIX A.

(*Translation.*)

CHAMARTIN,
December 10, 1808.

MARSHAL DUKE OF DALMATIA,

I read to the Emperor your letter of the 4th December, which was brought by one of your officers. His Majesty approves of all you have done. The 8th Regiment of Dragoons, the 22nd Chasseurs, the Regiment of Colonel Tascher, and the Hanoverian Regiment, form two brigades, commanded by the Generals Debelle and Franceschi. These two brigades are under your orders, and you can manœuvre them as you think proper. The Emperor is of opinion that with the Division of Merle and the Division of Mouton, together with the four regiments of cavalry, nothing can resist you.

What have you to do? Take possession of Leon, drive back the enemy into Galicia, make yourself master of Benevente and Zamora.

You can have no English in your front, for some of

215

their regiments came to the Escurial and Salamanca, and everything evinces they are in full retreat.

Our advanced guard is this day at Talavera de la Reyna, upon the road to Badajos, which it will reach soon. You clearly perceive that this movement must compel the English to hasten immediately to Lisbon, if they are not gone there already. The moment, Marshal, you are sure that the English have retreated, of which there is every presumption, move forward with rapidity. There are no Spaniards who can resist your two divisions. Order shoes and greatcoats to be made at Leon, St. Andero, and Palencia. His Majesty grants every demand for improving your equipment. You may also require mules for your artillery, and horses to remount your cavalry; but let it be all done according to the regular forms of administration.

It is possible that, as soon as the dragoons of General Millar shall arrive in Spain, the Emperor will send them to you; but this cannot happen these fifteen days. At the distance you are, Marshal Duke, you must direct yourself, and look upon all I write as only general instructions. His Majesty imagines that you will take every measure to reduce the country between the Duero, Galicia, and the Asturias, always preserving most attentively St. Andero.

The 5th Corps, commanded by the Marshal Duke of Treviso, has received an order to direct its march to Saragossa. The 8th Corps, under the Duke of Abrantes, whose 1st Division arrived at Vittoria on the 12th, will probably receive orders to unite at Burgos. Gunboats and armed vessels of every kind have orders to sail to St. Andero. Load them with confiscated English merchandise — cotton, wool, artillery (*sic*) — and send all to France.

In short, hold Valladolid and Zamora in subjection. Valladolid is a good town, which has behaved well. It is thought to be very important to occupy Zamora. To conclude, the Emperor thinks that you can do what you please as soon as the English retire to Lisbon.

Five divisions of Castaños' best troops have been routed with even less difficulty than you found in beating the Andalusian* army at Burgos.

The wreck of Castaños' army is pursued by Marshal Bessières, who has cut them off from the road to Estremadura, and is pursuing them towards Valentia, several marches beyond the Tagus. The Emperor's headquarters are at Chamartin, a little country seat a league and a half from Madrid. His Majesty enjoys an excellent state of health.

The city of Madrid is quite tranquil ; the shops are all open, the public amusements are resumed, and there is not the least appearance of the first proposals having been strengthened by 4,000 cannon-balls.

THE PRINCE OF NEUFCHÂTEL, M.G.

I will send you to-morrow a Proclamation and some Decrees of the Emperor, in which you will recognize the style of him who was born to command the world.

* *Note by the writer of the Journal :* "Mistaken for the Estremaduran army."

APPENDIX B.

GENERAL ORDERS.

HEADQUARTERS,
SAHAGUN,
December 22, 1808.

The different attacks made by the cavalry upon those
of the enemy during the march have given them the
opportunity to display their address and spirit, and to
assume a superiority which does them credit, and which
the Commander of the Forces trusts will be supported
upon more important occasions.

The attacks conducted by Brigadier - General the
Honourable Charles Stewart and the 18th Light Dragoons,
when upon the Duero ; and that by Lieutenant-General
Lord Paget, upon the enemy's cavalry at this place, are
honourable to the British cavalry.

The Commander of the Forces begs that the Lieutenant-
General and Brigadier-General will accept his thanks for
these services ; and that they will convey them to Brigadier-
General Slade, and the officers, non-commissioned officers,
and men of the cavalry, under their command, for their
conduct in the different affairs which have taken place.

APPENDIX C.

GENERAL ORDERS.

HEADQUARTERS,
SAHAGUN,
December 23, 1808.

The army will march in two columns by the right this
evening, and is to be formed in close column of sections

of five or six files; the cavalry by twos, clear of the cantonments, upon the road which will be pointed out by the Assistant-Quartermaster-Generals of Divisions, at eight o'clock, in the following order :

RIGHT COLUMN.

One Squadron of 3rd Light Dragoons, K.G.L. ⎫
Second Flank Brigade ⎪ Advance
Half-Troop of Horse Artillery ⎬ Guard.
3rd Light Dragoons, K.G.L. ⎪
Half-Troop of Horse Artillery ⎭

Lieutenant-General the Honourable John Hope's Division, with its Brigade of Artillery.

LEFT COLUMN.

One Squadron of 7th Light Dragoons ⎫
First Flank Brigade ⎪ Advance
Half-Troop of Horse Artillery ⎬ Guard.
7th Light Dragoons ⎪
Half-Troop of Horse Artillery ⎭

Reserve, with its Brigade of Artillery.
Brigadier-General Slade's Brigade.
Lieutenant-General Sir David Baird's Division, with its Brigade of Artillery.

The spare ammunition waggons will follow their columns in the order of their respective brigades. The carts with regimental medical stores ; the mules with camp-kettles (such only as are required for carrying provisions for officers) in the order of their respective regiments. The entrenching tools attached to divisions will march with the brigades of artillery. The staff surgeons attached to divisions, with their equipment, will march in the rear of their divisions. The mules with regimental entrenching tools and surgeons' field-chests only are to march with the regiments. The rear-guard of each column will consist of a battalion and a squadron of cavalry. The army is to receive provisions for to-morrow, to be cooked this afternoon.

Those regiments which have been supplied with skins for carrying their wine will receive one day's allowance, and the Commissary is, if possible, to carry a day's allowance for the remainder.

The sick will be left in the cantonments of Sahagun, Grahal, and Villada, and be sent to-morrow morning to Sahagun, when the Inspector of Hospitals will make provision for their reception and will direct what medical aid will be left. A return of the sick of each division is to be sent to the Inspector of Hospitals as soon as possible. The baggage is also to be left in the present cantonments under a small guard, and be in readiness to follow to-morrow, on the order being sent. Lieutenant-Generals will be pleased to desire general officers commanding brigades, and officers commanding regiments, to direct the necessary precautions to be taken for preventing any confusion, or the possibility of any separation of the columns during the night march.

Major-General Manningham will direct one battalion of his brigade to remain at Sahagun, until further orders.

The extra reserve ammunition, over and above the ten rounds per man, in the possession of those regiments which joined the army with Lieutenant-General Sir David Baird, is to be delivered to the brigade of artillery, at two o'clock this day, in the Square of Sahagun. The mules which are allowed to march in the rear of the columns are solely for the purpose of carrying provisions for officers; and the Commander of the Forces desires that as few as possible may be so employed.

APPENDIX D.

GENERAL ORDERS.

HEADQUARTERS,
BENEVENTE,
December 27, 1808.

The Commander of the Forces has observed with concern the extreme bad conduct of the troops of late—at a moment when they are about to come in contact with the enemy, and when the greatest regularity and the best conduct are the most requisite. He is the more concerned at it, as till lately the behaviour of that part of the army, at least, which was under his own immediate command was so exemplary and did themselves so much honour.

The misbehaviour of the troops in the column which marched by Valderas to this place exceeds what he could have believed of British soldiers. It is disgraceful to the officers, as it strongly marks their negligence and inattention.

The Commander of the Forces refers to the General Orders of the 15th October and of the 11th November. He desires that they may be again read at the head of every company of the army: he can add nothing but his determination to execute them to the fullest extent. He can feel no mercy towards officers who neglect, in times like these, essential duties, or towards soldiers who disgrace their nation, by acts of villainy towards the country they are sent to protect. The Spanish forces have been overpowered; and until such time as they are reassembled, and ready again to come forward, the situation of this army must be arduous, and such as to call for the exertion of qualities the most rare and valuable in a military body. These are not bravery alone, but patience and constancy under fatigue and hardship, obedience to command, sober and orderly conduct, firmness and resolution in every different situation in which they may be placed. It is by the display of such qualities alone that the army can expect to deserve the name of soldiers; that they can be able to withstand the forces opposed to them, or to fulfil the expectations of their country.

It is impossible for the General to explain to his army the *motives* for the movements he directs. The Commander of the Forces can, however, assure the army that he has made none since he left Salamanca which he did not foresee, and was not prepared for; and, as far as he is a judge, they have answered the purposes for which they were intended.

When it is proper to fight a battle he will do it, and he will choose the time and place he thinks most fit: in the meantime he begs the officers and soldiers of the army to attend diligently to discharge *their* parts, and to leave to *him* and to the general officers the decision of measures which belong to them alone. The army may rest assured that he has nothing more at heart than their honour and that of his country.

APPENDIX E.

GENERAL ORDERS.

HEADQUARTERS,
ASTORGA,
December 30, 1808.

The present is a moment when the army is necessarily called upon to make great efforts and to submit to privations, the bearing cheerfully with which is a quality not less estimable than valour.

The good-will of the inhabitants will be particularly useful to the army, and can only be obtained by good conduct on the part of the troops.

The Commander of the Forces cannot impress too strongly on the whole army the necessity of this; and he trusts that the Generals and commanding officers will adopt such measures both on the march and in the cantonments as will insure it.

It is very probable that the army will shortly have to meet the enemy; and the Commander of the Forces has no doubt that they will eagerly imitate the worthy example which has been set them by the cavalry on several recent occasions, and particularly in the affair of yesterday, in which Brigadier-General Stewart, with an inferior force, charged and overthrew one of the best corps of cavalry in the French army.

The Generals will immediately inspect the baggage of the brigades and divisions. They are held responsible that it does not exceed the proportion fixed by the General Orders. In the future marches, the baggage and women belonging to each division are to precede the troops two hours; and Generals and commanding officers are held responsible that no articles of baggage whatever, except the surgeons' field-chests and entrenching tools, march with the troops. If any cart or mule carrying baggage shall be unable to keep pace with the column, the soldier in charge of it is to join his battalion immediately.

General officers commanding divisions will specify the strength of the baggage-guard, which is to be as limited as possible. The officer commanding the baggage-guard of the division will appoint a rear-guard, the officer of which is responsible that no soldier remains behind with baggage.

Commanding officers will direct that officers are quartered in the same houses with the soldiers.

APPENDIX F.

General Orders.

Headquarters,
Lugo,
January 6, 1809.

Generals and commanding officers of corps must be as sensible as the Commander of the Forces of the complete disorganization of the army.

The advanced guard of the French is already close to us, and it is to be presumed that the main body is not far distant: an action may therefore be hourly expected. If the Generals and commanding officers of regiments (feeling for the honour of their country and of the British arms) wish to give the army a fair chance of success, they will exert themselves to restore order and discipline in the regiments, brigades, and divisions, which they command.

The Commander of the Forces is tired of giving orders which are never attended to : he therefore appeals to the honour and feelings of the army he commands ; and if those are not sufficient to induce them to do their duty, he must despair of succeeding by any other means.

He was forced to order one soldier to be shot at Villa-franca, and he will order all others to be executed who are guilty of similar enormities : but he considers that there would be no occasion to proceed to such extremities if the officers did their duty ; as it is chiefly from their negligence, and from the want of proper regulations in the regiments, that crimes and irregularities are committed in quarters and upon the march.

Commanding officers will make a minute investigation of the state of their arms, accoutrements, and ammunition, and give directions for their being put into the best possible state for service which circumstances will allow.

Regiments are directed to send a sergeant to the main-guard, to receive stragglers who have been confined this day.

A return of the spare ammunition in possession of each battalion, over and above sixty rounds per man, to be immediately sent to the Adjutant-General's office, in the Cathedral Square.

APPENDIX G.

GENERAL ORDERS.

NEAR LUGO,
January 7, 1809.

The army must see that the moment is now come when, after the hardships and fatiguing marches they have undergone, they will have the opportunity of bringing the enemy to action. The Commander of the Forces has the most perfect confidence in their valour, and that it is only necessary to bring them to close contact with the enemy in order to defeat them; and a defeat, if it be complete, as he trusts it will be, will in a great measure end their labours.

The General has no other caution to give them, than not to throw away their fire at the enemy's skirmishers merely because they fire at them, but to reserve it till they can give it with effect.

APPENDIX H.

GENERAL ORDERS.

HEADQUARTERS,
LUGO,
January 8, 1809.

It is evident that the enemy will not fight this army, notwithstanding the superiority of his numbers, but will endeavour to harass and tease it upon its march.

The Commander of the Forces requests that it may be carefully explained to the soldiers that their safety depends solely upon their keeping their divisions and marching with their regiments; that those who stop in villages or straggle on the march will inevitably be cut off by the French cavalry, who have hitherto shown little mercy even to the feeble and infirm who have fallen into their hands.

The army has still eleven leagues to march : the soldiers must make an exertion to accomplish them ; the rear-guard cannot stop, and those who fall behind must take their fate.

APPENDIX I.

GENERAL ORDERS.

HEADQUARTERS,
BETANZOS,
January 10, 1809.

A great deal of irregularity has arisen from the practice of some commanding officers allowing soldiers, who pretend to be bad marchers, to precede their corps. Men of this description whom commanding officers may think it expedient to send forward must be placed under an officer, who is held responsible for their conduct.

Memorandum for General Officers.

To prevent the renewal of the same scene which the march of last night presented, the Commander of the Forces directs that, previously to the march to-morrow morning, the general officers will see their divisions and brigades properly formed ; that they wheel them by sections, and that during the march they pay constant attention to the preservation of that order.

APPENDIX J.

GENERAL ORDERS.

HEADQUARTERS,
CORUNNA,
January 16, 1809.

The Commander of the Forces directs that commanding officers of regiments will, as soon as possible after they embark, make themselves acquainted with the names of the ships in which the men of their regiments are embarked, both sick and convalescent; that they will state the number of sick present, also those left at different places; and mention at the back of the return where the men returned on command are employed.

APPENDIX K.

LETTER FROM SIR JOHN MOORE TO LORD CASTLEREAGH.

CORUNNA,
January 13, 1809.

MY LORD,

Situated as this army is at present, it is impossible for me to detail to your Lordship the events which have taken place since I had the honour to address you from Astorga on the 31st December. I have therefore determined to send to England Brigadier - General Charles Stewart, as the officer best qualified to give you every information you can want, both with respect to our actual situation and the events which have led to it. From his connection with your Lordship and with His Majesty's

Ministers, whatever he relates is most likely to be believed. He is a man in whose honour I have the most perfect reliance; he is incapable of stating anything but the truth, and it is the truth which at all times I wish to convey to your Lordship and to the King's Government.

Your Lordship knows that, had I followed my own opinion as a military man, I should have retired with the army from Salamanca. The Spanish armies were then beaten; there was no Spanish force to which we could unite, and, from the character of the Government and the disposition of the inhabitants, I was satisfied that no efforts would be made to aid us or favour the cause in which they were engaged. I was sensible, however, that the apathy and indifference of the Spaniards would never have been believed; that had the British been withdrawn the loss of the cause would have been imputed to their retreat; and it was necessary to risk this army to convince the people of England, as well as the rest of Europe, that the Spaniards had neither the power nor the inclination to make any effort for themselves.

It was for this reason that I made the march to Sahagun. As a diversion it succeeded. I brought the whole of the disposable force of the French against this army, and it has been allowed to follow it without a single movement being made, by any of what the Spaniards call armies, to favour my retreat.

The Marquis de la Romana was of no other use to me but to embarrass me by filling the roads by which I marched, with his cannon, his baggage, and his fugitives. The people of the Galicias, though armed, made no attempt to stop the passage of the French through their mountains. They abandoned their dwellings at

30

our approach, and drove away their carts, oxen, and
everything that could be of the smallest aid to the
army.   The consequence has been that our sick have
been left behind, and when our horses and mules failed
—which on such marches, and through such a country,
was the case to a great extent—baggage, ammunition,
stores, and even money, were necessarily destroyed or
abandoned.

I am sorry to say that the army, whose conduct I had
such reason to extol on its march through Portugal and
on its arrival in Spain, has totally changed its character
since it began to retreat.   I could not have believed, had
I not witnessed it, that a British army could in so short a
time have been so completely disorganized.   Its conduct
during the late marches has been infamous beyond belief.
I can say nothing in its favour but that, when there was a
prospect of fighting the enemy, the men were then orderly,
and seemed pleased and determined to do their duty.   In
front of Villafranca the French came up with the Reserve,
with which I was covering the retreat of the army.
They attacked it at Cacabelos.   I retired covered by the
95th Regiment, and marched that night to Herrerias, and
thence to Nogales and Lugo, where I had ordered the
different divisions which preceded to halt and collect.   At
Lugo the French again came up with us; they attacked
our advanced posts on the 6th and 7th, and were repulsed
in both attempts, with little loss on our side.

I heard from the prisoners taken that three divisions of
the French army were come up, commanded by Marshal
Soult.   I therefore expected to be attacked on the morning
of the 8th.   It was my wish to come to that issue.   I had
perfect confidence in the valour of the troops, and it was

only by crippling the enemy that we could hope either to retreat or to embark unmolested. I made every preparation to receive the attack, and drew out the army in the morning to offer battle. This was not Marshal Soult's object. He either did not think himself sufficiently strong, or he wished to play a surer game by attacking us on our march or during our embarkation. The country was intersected, and his position too strong for me to attack with an inferior force.

The want of provisions would not enable me to wait longer. I marched that night, and in two forced marches, bivouacking for six or eight hours in the rain, I reached Betanzos on the 10th instant. The stragglers of the army amounted to many thousands, occasioned partly by the length of the marches, which in bad weather many men were unable to support; the want of shoes, hundreds being barefoot; and many left their ranks who had not so good an excuse, but from a desire to plunder. As the army was followed by the French cavalry, a great number of the above descriptions fell into their hands.

At Lugo I was sensible of the impossibility of reaching Vigo, which was at too great a distance, and offered no advantages to embark in the face of an enemy. My intention then was to have retreated to the peninsula of Betanzos, where I hoped to find a position to cover the embarkation of the enemy in Ares or Rodes Bays; but having sent an officer to reconnoitre it, by his report I was determined to prefer this place. I gave notice to the Admiral of my intention, and begged that the transports might be brought to Corunna. Had I found them here on my arrival on the 11th, the embarkation would easily have been effected, for I had gained several marches on the French. They have now come up with us; the transports are not arrived; my position in front of this place is a very bad one, and this place, if I am forced to retire into it, is commanded within musket-shot, and the harbour will be so commanded by cannon on the coast that no ship will be able to lie in it. In short, my Lord, General Stewart will inform you how critical our situation is. It has been recommended to me to make a proposal to the enemy to induce him to allow us to embark quietly; in which case he gets us out of the country soon, and this place with its stores, etc., complete, that otherwise we have the power to make a long defence, which must insure the destruction of the town. I am averse to make any such proposal, and am exceedingly doubtful if it would be attended with any good effect; but whatever I resolve on this head, I hope your Lordship will rest assured that I shall accept no terms that are in the least dishonourable to the army or to the country.

I find I have been led into greater length and more detail than I thought I should have had time for: I have written under interruptions, and with my mind much occupied with other matter. My letter written so carelessly can only be considered as private; when I have more leisure I shall write more correctly. In the meantime I rely on General Stewart for giving your Lordship the information and detail which I have omitted.

I should regret his absence, for his services have been very distinguished; but the state of his eyes makes it impossible for him to serve, and this country is not one in which cavalry can be of much use.

If I succeed in embarking the army. I shall send it to England—it is quite unfit for further service until it has been refitted, which can best be done there; and I cannot think, after what has happened, that there can be any intention of sending a British force again into Spain.

I have the honour to be, etc.,

(Signed)   JOHN MOORE.

APPENDIX L.

ROUTE OF THE BRITISH CAVALRY, UNDER THE COMMAND OF LORD PAGET, DURING THE CAMPAIGN IN SPAIN, 1808-09.

	Spanish Leagues.
Corunna to Betanzos	3
Betanzos to Monte Salguero	3
Monte Salguero to Gutoriez	2
Gutoriez to Bamondé	2
Bamondé to Lugo	4
Lugo to Constantino	4
Constantino to Las Nogales	4
Las Nogales to Trabadelos	7
Trabadelos to Cacabelos	4
Cacabelos to Bembibere	5
Bembibere to Astorga	8
Astorga to La Bañeza	4
La Bañeza to Benevente	6
Benevente to Zamora	12
Zamora to Toro	6
Toro to Morales	1
Morales to Tordesillãs	5
Tordesillãs to La Motta	4
La Motta to Villalpando	11

			Spanish Leagues.
Villalpando to Mayorga	...	...	... 8
Mayorga to Sahagun	...	...	... 8
Sahagun to St. Nicolas	...	...	... 4
St. Nicolas to Sahagun	...	...	... 4
Sahagun to Valderas ...	...	...	... 9
Valderas to Villa Guexida	...	...	... 10
Villa Guexida to La Bañeza ...	...	...	... 6
La Bañeza to Astorga	...	...	... 4
Astorga to Mansañassa	...	...	... 8
Mansañassa to Villafranca	...	...	... 7
Villafranca to Lugo ...	...	...	... 17
Lugo to Gutoriez	...	...	... 6
Gutoriez to Betanzos	...	...	... 5
Betanzos to Corunna	...	...	... 3
Total	...	...	194

APPENDIX M.

LIST OF THE OFFICERS OF THE 15TH (OR KING'S) HUSSARS
WHO SERVED IN THE CAMPAIGN OF 1808-09.

Lieutenant-Colonel Colquhoun Grant.
Major Francis Forrester.
Major W. N. Leitch.
Captain J. Broadhurst.
Captain E. McGregor Murray.
Captain L. C. Dalrymple.
Captain Edwin Griffith.
Captain Hon. W. E. Cochrane.

Captain Josephus Seelinger.
Captain Joseph Thackwell.
Captain Alexander Gordon.
Lieutenant John Buckley.
Lieutenant Skinner Hancox.
Lieutenant Baron L. During.
Lieutenant John Whiteford.
Lieutenant Edward Knight.
Lieutenant John Penrice.
Lieutenant Lewis Jones.
Lieutenant Charles Jones (Adjutant).
Lieutenant Charles Carpenter.
Cornet S. Jenkins.
Cornet James Laroche.
Cornet Frederick Phillips.

Staff.

Paymaster ...	... Richard Henslow.
Surgeon ...	... W. Lidderdale.
Assistant Surgeon	... John Forbes.
Veterinary Surgeon	... James Castley.
Adjutant ...	... Charles Jones (Lieutenant).

Right Squadron.

Squadron Leader	... Major Forrester.
Right Troop ...	... Captain Seelinger's.
Left Troop ...	... Captain Thackwell's.

Right Centre Squadron.

Squadron Leader	... Captain Broadhurst.
Right Troop ...	... Captain Broadhurst's.
Left Troop ...	... Captain Dalrymple's.

Left Centre Squadron.

Squadron Leader	...	Captain Murray.
Right Troop	...	... Captain Murray's.
Left Troop	...	... Captain Cochrane's.

Left Squadron.

Squadron Leader	...	Major Leitch.
Right Troop	...	... Captain Griffith's.
Left Troop	...	... Captain Gordon's.

INDEX

237

THE END

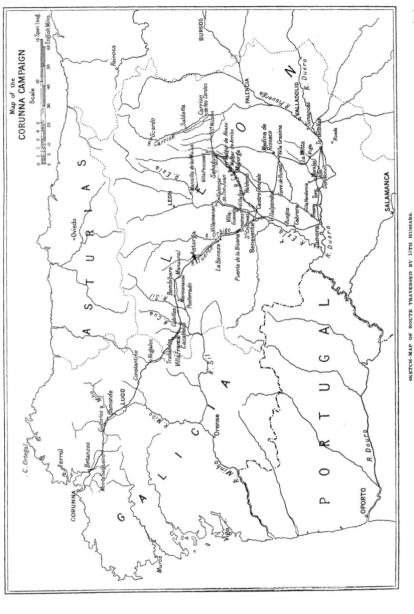

SKETCH-MAP OF ROUTE TRAVERSED BY 15TH HUSSARS.